THE JOURNALS OF TWO POOR DISSENTERS

WILLIAM SWAN
1813–1880

THE JOURNALS OF
TWO POOR DISSENTERS
1786—1880

Preface by
GUIDA SWAN

Introduction by
JOHN HOLLOWAY

LONDON: ROUTLEDGE & KEGAN PAUL

First published 1970 by Routledge & Kegan Paul Limited
Broadway House, 68–74 Carter Lane, London, E.C.4.

© Guida Swan 1970

Printed in Great Britain by
Alden & Mowbray Ltd at the Alden Press, Oxford

ISBN 0 7100 6673 2

Contents

Preface

The Journals, two worn and grubby-looking little books, full of faded, spidery handwriting, were first shown to me in 1947. I remember that an elderly maiden-aunt, living rather in the manner of a character from *Cranford* in her Garden City cottage, gave them to my husband. She was a descendant of that grandson William (in the second Journal) who went to live in Manchester.

Her brother was my father-in-law, the Reverend F. R. Swan, but he and I never met. We think that he never knew of the Journals, although his lively conscience led him to work in similar surroundings in London. He was a Nonconformist clergyman working with R. J. Campbell at the City Temple, and later was Minister of the Brotherhood Church in Southgate Road, where his pulpit was once set on fire by those who disapproved of his views – he had invited Bertrand Russell to speak from it, during the First World War.

Reading the Journals first in my youth, I felt, I suppose, that rebellion against poverty I could understand, and escape from poverty by individual heroic effort as in romantic fiction, I could admire, but the dreary, sour taste of continuing and accepted poverty was something I did not wish to dwell upon. I skipped through the manuscripts, hoping for a turning point towards wit, gaiety, worldly success. Twenty years later I still remembered their flavour and yet in re-reading them and editing their Biblical references, I came to appreciate the validity, for the writers, of their religious faith, so painfully upheld under that taunt of 'How can God love you that has made you a cripple for life?', so confident, through hardship, of their individual worth to God; and one might concede that even the dour, grim Puritanism helped them to keep their families on the living side of starvation.

Dr. John Holloway has written very much what I felt to be true as I re-read the Journals, and I am most grateful for his thoughtful Introduction to them.

GUIDA SWAN

Introduction

It will not take long to read this little book, and those who
read it hastily may see little in it. But they are likely to find
that it comes back to mind, and intrigues them until they
read it again and ponder it. Then they will see it differently.
The two authors, father and son, were working men, one
of the early and the other of the mid-nineteenth century.
Both lived in the poorer quarters of East London – Stepney,
Stratford, Stoke Newington – places which lay rather
beyond the usual perspective of a novelist like Dickens,
or a visitor to London, in the son's middle age, like Hippo-
lyte Taine. From the great sea of anonymity – London of
the nineteenth-century poor – come these two voices, brief
and plain and staid, but moving and true as well.

The father, William Thomas Swan, was born in 1786,
and in early life was a bricklayer (though perhaps not a fully
skilled one), then a porter at Billingsgate fish market and a
corn meter, whose task it was to weigh corn before it was
discharged from shipping. The grandfather owned house-
property, though it seems only on a small scale, and was
a member of the Church of England. But in 1803, the year
when war was renewed between Great Britain and Bona-
parte, a Calvinist 'track' was put into William's hand as he
walked down the street one Sunday. This began what he
calls 'my warfare with my father', and within a year or so
he was obliged to break with his family and to leave home.

A few years later, in 1811, he went a step further, and joined a strict or 'particular' Baptist congregation. Thus, in spite of being a fellowship porter, he does not much recall the 'Six Jolly Fellowship Porters' which was the scene of much conviviality in *Our Mutual Friend*; and his narrative also gives a very different picture of the porter's life from what may be glimpsed in the pages of Mayhew's *London Life and Labour*. In later life William Thomas fell from an omnibus near the West India Docks, and was more or less a permanent semi-invalid.

William Swan, born when his father was twenty-seven, was apprenticed to a confectioner (that is, a maker of cakes) in Stratford, Essex, which by this time was already part of London. But his apprenticeship seems to have been unsatisfactory, and he suffered throughout his life from injury and ill-health. Moreover, the father, at least before his accident, was 'one of the most cheerful and happy men in the world'. The son does not sound like this at all. He was asthmatic; perhaps his vitality was low and he was inclined to be querulous; and he himself records that his brother 'did not like my company' (this brother, though, was the black sheep of the family). None of his six children had him at their weddings ('my presence not being desirable'). His recurrent attacks of scurvy and other rather uninviting ailments suggest that he was the victim, psychologically as well as physiologically no doubt, of the poor conditions of life and diet and the inadequate medicine of the time. One sees a kind of dull, featureless tragedy in the inevitable consequence: he was almost never given a chance to work at his trade save intermittently, when business was especially brisk or someone else was ill; and while his father's later years seem to have been spent in modest prosperity, he himself spent most of his life, and especially the later part of it, near to real want. Between them, father and son take the narrative down to 1880. Then the son dies and the story comes to an end.

From their own point of view, their lives were not uneventful. For them, to begin with, the ill-health and physical mishaps which dogged both their lives must have been dramatic and momentous things, threatening them sharply (and one senses this well enough from time to time) with starvation. 'We could feed the children', William Swan writes, without adornment, of a time when life was less hard than usual. Today one is slow to realize how, in those times, and indeed long after, mere survival, mere ability to go on working and avoid the plunge into destitution, was a great achievement. Besides this, since nearness to work was vitally important, and their belongings must have been few enough, the Swans moved house very frequently, and these changes would have seemed momentous although they were often no more than from one modest little street to the next. Much of where they lived and worshipped has been swept away, but in several places (often surrounded by grandiose modern buildings, or by the roar and dust of demolition) the terraces in which both father and son lived may still be seen.

The lives of these two men were eventful also, to some degree, in a more conventional sense. William Thomas, as I said, began adult life with a serious breach between himself and his father, and with being – if it is not too grand a word – disinherited. One of his sons (not William Swan) stole from his father by forgery, and on some other matter had to be rescued at the last minute from the Old Bailey. This at least is what William Thomas's account tells us.

William Thomas also quarrelled badly, over some years it seems, with his only sister. As for William Swan, the fact that both he and his 'sweetheart' were strict Baptists did not prevent them from producing an illegitimate child ('Ah, this brought guilt into my conscience . . . I used to think there could be no mercy for me'). They had enough money to marry only by the time the child was three years old. Later, their eldest son, clearly a young man of talent, who went into an office and earned a substantial salary, several times seems to have refused help to his father in want, and also took to drink and died at an early age. Two of the sons, in fact, wormed their way out of giving a pittance to their father in his old age.

So these two lives had in them what could perhaps have made a much more dramatic narrative than the one we have. This did not happen, because William Thomas and his son were men of a certain kind, and had their own view of what was important in their lives, and worthy of prominence in their narratives. They had no idea of impressing or exciting. They do not seem to have found their own wrong-doings (if it is the word), nor those of others, in the least intriguing or zestful; but occasions only for grief, penitence or admonishment. They were by no means typical of the East London working class of their time; and several passages, in both narratives, make it clear that among all the men they worked with, there was scarcely one who shared their religious life. I do not think that this life can by any means be praised without reserve. Certainly, in its general colour, there was something wan and dreary which made it a very imperfect counterweight to the life of physical dreariness and deprivation which the Swans had to lead. Perhaps also there are hints of self-righteousness or niggling censoriousness. That was common enough at the time, as one knows; but when one reads that the younger Mrs. Swan insisted on going out to work as a washerwoman, 'but alas! . . . in going out there was a sad habit acquired of taking strong drink', one does not escape the feeling that in her autobiography there might have been a gaiety lacking to this one.

Happiness, though, is not altogether lacking. The Swans very seldom gave themselves anything by way of a 'treat' (the father records going to the 1851 Great Exhibition after it had been moved to the Crystal Palace). But we see the sedate – if not entirely sedate – joys of the younger Swan with his sweetheart Harriet Glass, 'the picture of health and cleanliness'; then, towards the end of each narrative, one can glimpse the companionship that old married couples, in spite of want and illness, can bring each other; and in the middle years, '. . . now my lads began to get little places between school hours, which was helping to us . . . these were among the happiest days of my fleeting life, when the children gathered round and we sung and conversed and sometimes prayed with them. Peaceful happy Sabbaths we had.' Yet one sees with pain, even in those words, how the writer barely looked for happiness save on one day in the week. One cannot call William Swan an uncomplaining man, but his life was governed by a large acceptance which we do not know today, but can wonder at and, I think, admire. 'She returned in health. Surely the mercies of the Lord . . . attend his household all their days.' That is the end of a paragraph. The next one opens 'Had no work this month.' So much, one thinks, for the constant attendance of the Lord's mercies; but the writer was more forbearing.

There is perhaps another reason, though of course a related one, why these two narratives are never dramatic or exciting in tone. The authors were plain working men, and in the main their language is plain and bald. 'A very severe winter when there was very little doing anywhere'; '. . . my wife took to her bed . . . she lingered till the third of May, and died in peace'; 'had no work this month, except half a day at the bread baker's, but it was very plain'. In this respect as in others, the father's narrative and the son's are very much the same: they represented a single continuing way of life, limited and recessive but self-contained and inwardly strong, which lasted on, in the corners of our society, beyond their time and probably until the Second World War. When the writing acquires a more resonant note, the English of the Authorized Version, and of the dissenting hymns and metrical psalms which came out of it, is never far away. But this language was largely one with the enduring common speech of the people; and it is that which plays its part also, when the style becomes incisive and memorable: '. . . they drove on with the affair and managed to clap him in office. . . . He was the most coarse and uneducated man I ever heard presume to speak from a pulpit.' In this crisper note, but also in the clean plainness, like scrubbed wood, of the whole, one can see a quality that gives this book a real if modest place in our literature. Its values, of style as of life, make up a soundness which today most of us barely know, and which deserve to be held in regard when the fashionable style of more sophisticated writers has long been brushed aside.

JOHN HOLLOWAY

Note on the text

Apart from a few minor alterations in punctuation, the text has been left as it stands in the manuscript, and the original spelling has been retained as a feature of the work.

The Journal of
WILLIAM THOMAS SWAN

born 1786

1841. *July* 31.

'Thou shalt look back on all the way the Lord thy God hath led thee, this forty years in the wilderness.'

Actuated by this truth, and in order to my own profit and the profit of others, – having a good deal of spare time, – I thus look back to the time when the Lord began a good work upon my heart.

I think I was about seventeen, about 1803, when on a Sabbath day, walking out with a young man to whom I was much attached, a person put a track in my hand, which I took care off and read afterward, – but I don't recollect the exact effect. But this was partly owing to my friends dog running down a fowl, which my companion put in his pocket, and took and eat at a house which he and I used to go to, – but after this I never went more, no, not to partake of it.

About this same time, my wicked thoughts began to be a trouble to me, for altho I had been brought up strictly moral, and watched over by parents, so that I thought many times too strictly, yet I gave way to swearing and every other vice in their absence. Especially so when driven from

B   I

home for base conduct, I was employed among men at the building of the first Tobacco warehouse in the London Docks as a bricklayer, – though I was not proficient. Here I became so vile that one day a professor reprov'd me, which had a good effect. Another time going home sensibly drunk, my mother was helping me up to bed and she being in tears, I told her not to weep, – I would take a turn, which did take place while we were in that house.

And so it was one Sabbath day, being at St. George's Church, (for we liv'd in that parish then), Mr. Blenkarne preach'd from these words, –

'So teach us to number our days that we may apply our hearts to wisdom.'

From this he showed that all the wisdom in the world was very good in its place, but not to be compared with the wisdom contained in the scriptures, and exhorted to a constant reading of them.

Now it was that I had been always forc'd to go to church, and I suppose twelve months or more before this, I remember being very desirous to have my mind disengag'd from everything else when engag'd in the worship of God, but yet continued in sin.

However after hearing Mr. Blenkarne, I was led to read my Bible, and to refrain from sin, by degrees. I got very Pharissaic, but in due time was led to Christ, though I laboured under conviction I know not how long.

The first sacred truth I ever agreed with was, – 'The heart is deceitful and desparately wicked', which I had proof of by the horrid Temptations to blaspheme the Name of God.

So harassed was I, that one night after going to bed, the Devil was wont to persuade me that I had done it, and he would carry me away, out of the window. But blessed be to God, the Spirit, He taught me that 'we are not bound and tied by the chains of our sins . . .'

'O God, to whom all hearts are open, all desires known, and from whom no secrets are hid, cleanse the thoughts of our hearts by the inspiration of thy Holy Spirit that we may perfectly love thee, and worthily magnify thy Name, through Jesus Christ, our Lord. Amen.'

Thus for a long time I went on, sinning, and repenting and crying to the Lord, till by the effectual working of God's mighty power, I was brought to see myself as altogether helpless and hopeless.

But as this was discovered to me so was the ability and willingness of Christ to save revealed to me.

Also the blessed Spirit taught me the length and breadth, and the spirituality of his law, and that there was no more contain'd therein than he had a just right to demand of us. So that the law became like a Schoolmaster to bring me to Christ.

One evening, returning from Sion Chapel, when opposite Whitechapel workhouse, (for we had mov'd then to Stepney Green), readdy to perish in my own apprehension, and thinking that my next step would be into Hell, – the eye of my mind was lifted up to Jesus as being seated at the right hand of the Father.

All at once it was as if a voice spoke peace to me, which took away all my fears, and burdens and brake the bonds of my yoke and delivered me from the powers of darkness.

I was filled with joy and peace in my soul, and had a wish to die directly rather than live to sin against so good a God. These words were uppermost in my mind, – 'Lord, lettest now thy servant depart in peace, for my eyes have seen thy salvation.'

Then it occur'd to me that I needs must live to fulfill my generation, then again I was willing to wait my appointed time.

I think it was the same evening that I read the parable of the prodigal son, and when I came to that part, – 'And when he saw him a great way off, he ran and fell upon his neck and kissed him', – I was so overcome with a view of God's readyness to forgive and receive the returning sinner that I could not go on. My mother was much surprised, but knew nothing of what was passing in my mind, altho a change was so evident.

I continued to attend Sion Chapel because the Church prayers were read there, and I thought my father would not mind so much my going there as to a Dissenters where they were not read.

I was now between 17 and 18 years old. When I was forc'd to go to Stepney Church with my brothers it was a barren time for me. So began my warfare with my father. My father said I was getting righteous overmuch and wanted to teach him. About this time these words were applied, – 'He that loveth father and mother more than me is not worthy of me.'

I was led to make it a matter of prayer to be delivered from my fathers hand that I might serve the Lord more freely.

Now my father did frequently threaten me, if I persisted in this course I should never be the better for what he was possess'd of. But blessed be to God, I have lived to prove 'He can restore what we resign or grant us favours more divine'.

Notwithstanding his threats, by the grace of God, I was helped to resign all claim on my father, also about twenty pounds I had saved out of labour under Pomfret.

After being driven from home, out to seek work before, I knew my business. But God led me to a man who had liv'd in one of my father's houses, a Taskmaster in London Docks. This man behaved in many respects like a father, instructed me, and paid me, and took great pride in me. This I look back upon as a providence, – (excepting that here I had learnt to drink, swear etc.)

But to return to my experience, – when I was willing to part with all for Christ, and wanted to get from under my father's roof that I might serve God more fully and freely, accordingly I made it a matter of prayer. In answer to which, one Sunday morning, coming down stairs to go to a Lecture at the back of the Bank where Mr. Gunn, Mr. Draper, and Mr. Saunders preach'd, (this service commenc'd at six) my father came out of his room saying, – 'If you will persist in this way you had better seek a lodging elsewhere.'

No one knows how this gladden'd my heart, and cheerfully I went to the back of the Bank, where I met with my friend, G. Laker, a Journeyman bricklayer, who had told me of this Lecture. When I told him, he was as glad as me, and took me to his lodgings where I lodg'd for some time, in Nightingale Lane.

Next day I went home for my clothes. My father was not at home, nor did I see him again for a long time. My mother said she thought I was going to be married. 'O No,' said I, 'If I continue in this same mind, I shall never be married.' For the force of the words of the Apostle I felt, – 'He that is married careth for the things of this world, how he may please his wife.'

What a marvellous change was here! I suppose 12 or 18 months before very few were more carnal sensual and devilish, –Oh to grace how great a debtor!

Now when I took my box of clothes the landlady said it would not be for long, but blessed be to God, I never regretted, nor had a wish to return home.

My new friends were members of Mr. Nicholson's Mulberry Gardens Chapel, Pell Street, at which place I attended sometimes, but chiefly I went to Sion Chapel to which place I was much attached because there I had some of the first and the brightest displays of God's goodness in the forgiveness of sins and of man's redemption.

But Mr. Nicholson had been brought up to the church and I needs must hear him. Besides, an old school fellow liv'd near my lodging who was a member, and with him I us'd to have a good Christian conversation, and by him I was introduced to be a teacher in their Sunday school, – this in perhaps six or seven months.

In 1805 or 6 I began to feel somewhat uncomfortable in my lodgings, partly thro my Landlord and Lady not being comfortable to each other, upon which I said to my school fellow I thought I should seek a wife.

Now he had engaged to get me a pair of razors. Accordingly one evening I went to see if he had got them, and went into the Shop. My wife was standing there. She was begging for some female in distress. From this our acquaintance commenced and about three or four months after we was married, – in January 1807.

My wife, being a member of Mr. Hyatts at Ebenezer Chapel, Shadwell, Independents, – of course I attended there, and in a very little time became a member. This connexion brought me into intimate acquaintance with a member whose name will ever be dear to me, – Jacob Martell, a friend of my wife's, insomuch that he was a means in the hand of God of reviving my poor soul which was in a backsliding state in that I gave way to a light and troubling spirit.

Never shall I forget the searching and instructing effect of his conversation and that his preaching and prayers had on me. It was he who first took me to a social prayer meeting. I look upon this part of my life as being very important next to my conversion.

Soon after my marriage, a Mr. Blackburn started a sunday school in Pennington Street, called then in 1807, the Protestant Sunday School. This was the origin of the school at Hyatts. To this I was invited to assist as having been a teacher at Mr. Nicholson's. With this and my diligence in the use of means, I became very much esteemed, which thing became a very great snare to me. I was very proud of it, till at length the Lord convinc'd me of this Evil by suffering me to fall into worldly trouble to such a depth that had it not been for a member of Mr. Stodharts I must have gone to Jail.

But by his kindness, and by selling off scaffolding and nearly everything that would fetch a guinea, it cleared my way a little. I retired to one room and to Journeywork. After a while my Christian friends subscribed together and helped and raised me enough to take up my Freedom and Fellowship, to which employment I went to work in 1811 at Billingsgate, and anywhere and everywhere, to get myself out of debt. I was a long time so doing.

In the beginning of this trouble how did I kick like a bullock unaccustomed to the yoke! Till one evening at Ebenezer Chapel, Mr. Hyatt said something about worldly trouble being brought on through love of the world, I was convinc'd that this was my case.

So much was I tossed and tempted at this time that I was, as it were, driven to a friend of mine at Clapham, to ask him for a place at one of his toll gates. Instead of this he set me about building two houses for him.

Also about this time I was led into a firm perssiasion of believers baptism, upon which I had a wish that others of Mr. Hyatts members should be baptised, the which when he heard of it, he paid me a visit and beg'd me if it was so, to withdraw quietly, and not take a multitude with me. He said there was a Mr. Shenstone in the district, he'd advice me to go there. . .

This was a time of great trouble. My Ebenezer friends said that I had involved myself in difficulties imprudently and seem'd to frown upon me, my nearest relatives gave it out I was excommunicated because I had left the Independents and attended the Baptists. So that I was in trouble in the World, in my Church, and in the family. But God was with me in all these troubles.

Thus I felt supported and sustained, struggling with difficulties and debts, and an increase in family.

After attending Mr. Shenstone's a while, I offer'd myself as a member, upon which, altho he was pleased with my experience and candid statements, he said he wished me to wait awhile, because I was in debt. However such was my attachment to his ministry and his people, I would not leave the place but attended every meeting I possibly could. Of an Ordinance day I sat in the gallery. Never shall I forget, one day, my bitterness of soul when returning home from there I was readdy to exclaim, 'No man careth for my soul.'

Yet I was enabled to hold on, looking within on myself as unworthy to have a place among a holy people.

So I waited about a Twelvemonth and then Mr. Shenstone was again propos'd to visit, – he admitted me. I was one of the first to be baptised in our own Baptistry. A blessed occasion with a blessed sermon from John, chapter 14, verse 21. 'He that hath my commandments and keepeth them . . .'

When I look back over the toils and snares of this time,– about 1814, – I am a wonder to myself that I came safely through. I know I was a wonder to many, for such was my exertion at Billingsgate, shoring sprats, herrings and oysters, that one said, 'I give you seven years,' – but blessed be to God, this judgment was not correct.

By constant attendance early in the morning, when I could get a better job, Mr. Saunders' First Man would get me to bring the fish over the boats and up the ladder for him, and would give me half his money.

After a while this came to Mr. Saunders ears, and he took notice of me, gave me work occasionally, and after a while took me on, constant. And this too in a very severe winter when there was very little doing anywhere else. Here I was for three to four years, and a better master never was, so that I took great pleasure in his service and he shewed great favour towards me, – so much so that it incurr'd the jealousy of a fellow servant, a base fellow.

One morning, we was working barrell fish out of the Warehouse in Thames Street, when being near the corner of the Market, my foot slipt and I came down on my hip and bruised the joint. This fall I still feel, and shall, till my death.

But I still continued in the same place, till one morning,

having something to do in the warehouse, I fell foul of a fellow servant, whose father had been an old servant in the family, and being a very turbulent, wicked man had got the length of his master's foot.

He had for a long time manifested great hatred to me, and was very jealous because of favour shown to me, – also I had indulged a prejudice in my mind against him, to such a pitch that after a few words we got to blows. In consequence of which I was discharged, and he was kept on.

After a few days, I waited on Mr. Saunders, who said he had always been well pleased with my services and would do anything for me or mine. . . . This was a great loss, – constant employment, – and a sore trouble to me for some time. For being a young porter, and a professor, I found it hard to hold up my head.

After a while I bought a fish walk of a woman who went to America. I believe this was in the spring of 1817. Many a day, after walking many miles, I came home with little in pocket. In fact I think it is one of the hardest ways for an honest man to obtain a living.

Another thing I did was to take Price Currents to Merchants counting houses of a Friday evening.

Never shall I forget going along Moorfields pavement one evening, ruminating over the state I was in, and how it came about. The words of the Apostle came to my mind, – 'Charity thinketh no evil, is not easily provoked . . .' and I was led to see that as I had indulged in prejudice, thereby had I lost a good and constant place. Moreover I saw that God, in his goodness and long suffering bears and forbears with the wicked, so that it is our duty to bear and forbear too, and not to indulge in envy nor prejudice nor any evil disposition to them.

O what a humiliating effect it had on me, how I was humbled under the mighty hand of God that he should teach me to discover the cause of my present trouble! But this was a fulfilment of that saying, 'Unto the godly, there ariseth light in the darkness,' – which was my dawn of salvation.

Shortly after this I heard that there was some corn Meters to be made.

I sold my fish walk scales and basket, at very little loss, and applied to Mr. Saunders to recommend me to be a Corn Meter, which thing I obtained in November 1818, through the character he gave me, and the good providence of God raising me up friends where I thought I had none.

Yet I would not forget the kindness of our church members. The winter after I lost my place at Billingsgate ten shillings was given me by the deacons at Christmas 1817, and very acceptable it was.

Also when I obtained the Meters place, a friend, Mr. Alfie Battersby, lent me £5 to fray expenses, without interest.

I work'd at Billingsgate occasionally for my old Master and at corn work when I could get it.

A little while after I was made a Meter my father heard of it, filled with wonder how I obtained it, came to see me and invited us to his house. I went with my wife and family for Christmas 1819. This was very gratifying to me, especially as my father dyed suddenly the following summer.

After a while my mother offer'd me a house to live in, if I would do the repairs of the estate. This I undertook to do untill I found it to be to my disadvantage when I left her house and hired one. But what with increase of family and my being a young Meter I found it a hard matter to pay my way.

In about two years time she gave me a house to live in that had been empty for some time. By borrowing some money this was put in repair and we enter'd two and three quarter years before my mother's death, – which happened in 1835. In consequence of the houses not being insured, and some very out of repair, we agreed to sell them all.

'But he can restore what we resign
Or grant us favours more divine', –

now this was most strikingly fulfilled to my comfort when accomplished for the promise came to my mind, – 'The hand of the Lord shall be known towards his servants.'

On the day of the sale a Mr. Nash bought the six in Morgan Street, one of which I liv'd in and had helped to build when a boy. One day my father had said that he was building them for me.

But the day after the sale the Auctioneer sent for me to say I might have the six back, for Mr. Nash did not like his bargain. I see him the first opportunity when he told me he had alter'd his mind, for he had been to see them and found they was in better repair than he had expected. 'Well sir' said I, 'If you do part with them, I'll give you £10 for your bargain.'

At this he said 'See me again in a week', which I did, and went with him to the Lawyers to order the property to be transfer'd to me and at my expense. Notwithstanding which, I had £10 odd to take when everything was settled. Wonderful providence, – now much more use to me and my family has this been than the 170 guineas would have been. And moreover how wonderfull this providence in providing for my future crippled state, – but I have made a long digression.

Some time after joining the church, it so happened that I miss'd an old female, a Mrs. Benton, and finding that she was ill I went to see her so repeatedly that it came to Mr. Dean, a Deacon's ears. He soon afterwards said to me, 'I'll find you more of this work to do.' Shortly after this, Mr. Williams, who was then both Treasurer and Secretary of the Sick Mans Assistant Society, asked me to assist in Visiting. This was about the year 1820. At the resignation of Mr. W. I was called upon to be Secretary for a time but when our numbers were increas'd, a more efficient brother, Mr. White, took it on him.

O the felicity to be found in this service! I believe it to be a most important part of religion, to visit the fatherless and widows, the sick and distressed. And the more self-denial the more enjoyment in helping. O what scenes of distress have I seen in cellars and garretts and various places. Afflictions of such various kinds! Eyresepolis and Rhuematic gout where the features have been distorted to a frightful appearance, Paralysis where the use of the limbs and the speech has been so taken away that you could not make out what was said.

One of this sort was a man that we was told had been a very bad character, whose appearance was frightfull, and when he attempted to speak seemed to me to be all blasphemy. Another good woman with such a complication of complaints that she could not sit or lay long in one posture. Another speechless for years, but had her speech return just before her departure ... Another bed-ridden many years, but wonderfully supported by grace. Another with the spine of her back injured, and one with a cancered throat, such that there was a large hole in the throat for some time before she died. Again, Cancers ... and one case, very affecting, of a Bleeding Dropsy.

And accidents, – the one case I went to, where the man was very averse to hear anything good, but being requested by his wife, I went. I found him, sitting in a chair because his bed was being made. I was requested to wait. Meantime came in the Rev. Mr. Drake, and to our astonishment when they went to put him in bed, found that he had died in the chair.

O what ignorance have I seen! Truly, darkness covers the Earth, and gross darkness the people.

What bitterness in backsliders, what obstinacy and perverseness in infidels!

And one awful man, the husband of a good woman much afflicted, who still said he was safe, though living in sin. This man had been a Preacher, but to me it seemed as it were, as if he had the impress of Satan upon him, – and I make no doubt that some would be frighten'd at him. The vilest Antinomian I ever did see.

Another case, where the man would not see the first Visitor, but poor man, he listen'd to me and promis'd, very fair. He had imbibed false notions, and previous to this would not listen to sacred things.

But to return to my experience. In consequence of my large family, altho by my mother's death, I came to my little property, yet I work'd very hard, for my married children were very poor, and one very much afflicted, for seven years.

Yet, blessed be to God, I kept up a dilligent attendance on the means of grace, – tho some-times with much heaviness thro too much comformity to the world, and too much eagerness after worldly good, which brought on me much reproach and ill-will, and some-times shame and confusion in my soul. So that some-times at prayer meetings I have been afraid of being called upon. O what a narrow path is the path of a believer!

On 17th August 1839 I had been at work in the West India Docks and came up by an omnibus, when as I was getting down, my foot slip't and I fell on the hip, a tin box being in my pocket, coming between my hip and the stones. This laid me up for two weeks.

After this, I worked till the 11th August, 1840, on which day my hip bone appeared to be growing out, and was so inflamed that it was necessary to have Surgical advice. Accordingly a blister and medicine was ordered, and another in about ten days.

After this I went to Gravesend for a week, then I had three warm baths, – no better. In October I got Mr. Cory to give me a Surgeons Certificate to lay before the Corn Meters Fund Committee, – my case being incurable, a bruis'd hip joint.

And by this Certificate I have £60 a year. Bless'd be to God.

But this was a very trying time. I was like a man entering a dark cloud, I could not see through. I was at a loss to know how far I should do right by myself, my family and my Benefit society. I knew that flesh and blood loved ease, but on the other hand I was persuaded by what I felt, that I could not bear any exertion if I went to work.

If I went to work I should bring on inflammation. I was anxious to get a cure. I tried two pots of pomade at 4/6 a pot, but no use. After this, I went to Mr. Crichett in Broad Street, who bound up my thigh with plasters and several yards of bandages for three weeks. At the taking off of which, I see him again, but he was at a loss what to do, and was wont to persuade me to blister again, and talked of trying my constitution.

This I consulted my friends about, and Mr. Cory, – upon which he told me it was no use, that men of my age seldom get the better of this complaint.

Still anxious, I next tried brandy and salt, but in vain. Sometime after this, hearing of Cabburn's Oil 2/9 a bottle, after seeing Mr. Cabburn, I used three bottles, and I believe it removed the rheumatic pains which flew to that part, but the pain in the joint was, and is still the same. This then brings me to the Midsummer 1842, June 29th.

Two members of my benefit society waited on me to know if I would not relinquish my claim, because my general bodily health was good, and they thought I was capable of following light employ. Finding I would not, on the following Monday, at a Special Committee, they thought proper to stop my money. Upon this I went and left 10/- at the Secretary's house to call a Meeting of Arbitrators, which meeting took place at Surrey Chapel on July 22nd., the result of which was, – the Arbitrators justified the conduct of the Society for that no provision for lameness was made in any rule. I could remain a member, but I declined it.

The night after the deputation called from the Society, I had also two men call'd to say that if I did not pay £2. 16 shillings, my son, Thomas, would very likely be tried at the Old Bailey, – to prevent which I paid it, – unbeknownst to my wife.

My wife for months before had fallen off in mind and in memory, and gradually declined in bodyly health. She was under Dr. Rees three times, then rallied again, till the first of January 1842 when she kept her bed.

After this I was called upon to pay part of the pounds Tom owed for rent, and promised to give on from March, and at the same time was called upon for £3 for a new sewer in James Street, – paid it in August 1843. That same month had the houses painted outside for £6. 10. 0. and was forced to have three pairs of parlour shutters, cost near £3.

Having stated, – my wife took to her bed on the first day of January, and I go on to say that she was ill off and on till the middle of April, when, taking to her bed again, she lingered till the third of May, and died in peace. She was paralysed, but somewhat sensible the last four hours.

Mr. Dickerson improved the death of my Wife from the first chapter of Timothy 2, verse 12. My family were all present. She was interr'd at Mr. Hyatts on the 9th May 1843.

On the day of her death, or the day after, these words seemed to occupy my mind, – 'Art thou loosed from a wife? Seek not a wife.' which words I have since had different veins off, sometimes perhaps not to have another, sometimes perhaps, – to check my anxieties and eagerness.

But I never hope to forget the 16th June, when in a buss going to Newington to Dr. Fletcher's funeral, I thought, 'Sometimes the woman seeks the husband', – at which I felt happy in being at the entire disposal of God, and resigned to his will in this. I hope never to forget it.

The next important step was to seek reconciliation with my only sister, which took place on the 20th June, on the same day I visited a Mr. Dawson, and also followed Mr. Knowles to his grave, – and improved it among his

relations at his daughter's house. Returning home much
delighted with this promise, – 'They shall spend their days
in pleasure and their years in prosperity', – truly it was a
good day, blessed be to God.

June 24. 1843.

To-day I had conversation with a good woman, who had
formerly been with the Wesleys, but had seen so much she
thought wrong and inconsistent that for seven years she
had not entered a place of worship. She had been tempted
to make away with herself, and to think that there was no
God, nor any reallity in religion. But I doubt not she is a
vessel of mercy.

June 27.

Thinking of the words 'Seek not a wife', it came to my
mind that God is his own interpreter and he can make it
plain.

July 18.

I attended the annual meeting of the British Penitent Refuge
and their Asylum near the Canal Bridge, Cambridge Heath.
The effect of the speeches, – and so few there, – induced me
to take a Card to collect for them.

July 23. 1843.

The Lords Day. Heard Mr. D. preach on 'Called to be
Saints'. It had a very humiliating and blessed effect on me.
   Very poorly, and went to bed before tea, took some
Court drops, had some hot water to my feet and gruel for
supper, a dose of Courts mixture in the morning but stayed
at home all day, did not attend prayer meeting on Monday

night. With the trials and afflictions of the last year, I find it a world of tribulation. My family all so poor and I cannot do for them as I would.

'Lord help and comfort me, that my mind may be stayed on Thee, and my heart fixed on trusting Thee. Thou hast been my help, therefore under the shadow of thy wing will I rejoice. Amen.'

September.
Forc'd to commence paying £3. 10. od. for Margaret's husband by signing for him at 1/- per week. Early in November 7/6 for William, – but amidst it all, happy, under the means of grace. Having been a Meter 25 years this month the fund committee sent me ½ the advanced month's money, at the rate of £10 per year more.

In November two of our members died, making seven in six days to my cognizsance . . . all died hopefull.

January 5th 1844.
How can I have begun a New Period, without making some remarks of the mercies of God's covenant, by whose grace I have been sustained amidst all the conflicts of the past year. Lately I have wak'd with this blessed portion, – 'No good thing will be withheld from them that walk up-rightly.'

Another morning I had thoughts concerning the eating and drinking of the flesh and blood of Christ and was led to meditate on the various Ideas connected with this, also passages corroborating.

Altogether a blessed season, though much fatigued after visiting six afflicted dying people.

February 14. At Church meeting I had the happiness to hear my daughter Martha relate her experience before the Church, and she will be baptised on the last Sunday in February. O that she may follow on to know the Lord!

The last Saturday in July was the first time that I spoke to Mrs. Reynolds, – through her enquiring if my name was not Mr. Swan, at Mrs. Holliday's shop. This Circumstance I look'd upon as an answer to my anxieties, respecting the words, 'Seek not a wife', (this I was in doubt as to the meaning of it).

Previous to this, I had a secret wish to live in the locality where her house stands, and besides her daughter, Harriett sat down at Mr. Hyatts 1st Lord's Day, in March, the same day that my Martha did with us. The concurrence of these circumstances seemed to convince me that the hand of God is in it. 'Gracious God, if it is thy pleasure, make it evident more.'

About the latter end of March 1845 I heard that her eldest daughter was to be married in the course of the next month. Then thought I it expedient, that we should be married early in May, and when we talked about it, found we had both fixed on one day, the first Tuesday.

After this, I was very often in fear lest I should involve me in difficulties that would be a trouble to me. On Saturday the 6th, I thought I would try to let the house I liv'd in, on a lease. Next day felt very dull and stupid, but Monday came and at the prayer meeting in the evening, these words cheered me, – 'And can He have taught me to trust in his Name, and thus far have brought me to put me to shame?' Also the words, 'Thou art my expectation and my Hope.' And also our dear minister was led to say something about the same thing.

On the following Wednesday morning I wondered that I should doubt His love who has saved me in troubles past, but on the Sunday of May 5th, waking with the thoughts of the difficulties, and thraldrom I was entering upon, I was led to think of the blessed Lord who knew full well what a Cross of suffering He had to encounter, but He did not draw back. . . . Neither must I.

I was so overwhelmed with the tokens of my dear Lord's presence, and burst out saying, 'What manner of man OUGHT I to be?'

Astonishing are the oppositions we each have met with, from my family, her family, and some of the Lord's family. But blessed be to God for such helps as these through duty and through trial, looking at difficulties it has been as if the dear Lord said, – 'On me depend, I'm Jesus still, the sinner's Friend.' On May 7th we were married at Wickcliffe Chapel, by Mr. Stowell because Mr. Dickerson was dying. The day we was married we went to Gravesend for a week, was very comfortable, and well received by the friends at the Baptist Chapel there.

Witnessed the funeral of Mr. Dickerson on the 23rd at Sheen and after tea, visited two members known a long time to my wife, in an almshouse near Grove Rd, Bow Road.

Owing to it being a five week month it was a trying time, for besides our great expenses, I had to employ plumber, painter, glazier, carpenter, stenciller, locksmith and paper hanger. But notwithstanding all this I must record the goodness of God.

During the last month, my son, Tom, obtained ten shillings by forging my name. This was trying, but thinking it strange, I thought that there is nothing strange with God, and again looking forward, I thought 'What time I am afraid, I will trust in Him.'

For hoping that my mountain of difficulties will grow less as I approach them, am led to look back on times when It was so.

July 19. 1844.
This morning I am thinking of my circumstances and remember I could carry £1 in my pocket, and four year ago had £30 in the Savings Bank, but thro my eagerness, and conformity to the world, a judgment of God has fallen upon me, and now my hands are sealed so that I cannot do the things I would. 'Lord sanctify all and every circumstance, subdue my pride, and save me from walking in the vanity of my mind.'

September 11*th.*
Lately I have been led to think of the amazing goodness of God, He having done more and better than I asked. I only wished to live in this locality, and to be able to rent a house. He has given me a wife, and also a house, and that well-furnished. Blessed be to God, He helped me to pay £4 for Joseph (my son) ten days before it was due. He can make mountainous difficulties disappear the nearer we approach them. I fear I shall be forc'd to help Thomas and his family . . .

1844. *November 6th.*
Very much exercised in my mind with pecuniary matters, added to which Martha at home from Thomas's, – through carelessness and being a little pert.

The 7th . . . Had a helping hand in providence by receiving a month of Davis, – but on this day so relaxed that I did not go to meeting.

Ditto 8th. Still much relaxed and afraid to go out so that I sent for Dr. Cory.

After this, Martha was at home for 10 weeks and then went to hard service at Saint Mary Axe, – that was a trying time. Next thing I finished paying Mr. Hind the £3 10. 0. for Singleton but in January 1845 call'd upon to pay £2 16. 0 for him, part of £5, – unbeknownst to me, where I had gone surety for him.

March following, – Martha home again so ill. I got her a letter to be out patient at London Hospitall.

March 29th. Tom was troublesome again, said he'd get some money and I should pay for it on this day, – not a penny I could call my own.

May 15 1845. Paid the last of the money for Singleton. Martha been at West End at a better place in every respect, Blessed be to God. Have had my health better lately. Have had so much enjoyment of the divine presence lately, this morning while at breakfast it was as if the high praises of God were issuing out of my heart. But does not Scripture say 'Let the high praises of God be in their heart'?

My heart again filled with praise although these times I have need of patience and hope to see brighter days. I have not a shilling to call my own, and these five week months are very trying. But why should I talk of brighter days when thousands would be glad to be as I am, and again how many times have I been told that mine is an enviable situation.

April 24th 1846.
To-day I am 60 years old. What a mercy to be spar'd so long, and what a token for good, and many such tokens have I had, but not recorded them. However this being my birthday I must record it.

I waken'd out of one of the sweetest sleeps I ever had in my life and found I had been dreaming of being engag'd in prayer, communion and fellowship, so that I thought I was doubly refresh'd both with rest in sleep and from the visitation of grace. 'Verily, there is a reward for the righteous.'

In the evening of this day went to Eagle Street where was held the Strict Baptist Convention Association, – very few there, it was partly the formation of it.

May 1st, 1846.
Yesterday me and my dear Wife went to Exeter Hall, had much enjoyment, but wife had the sick headache again for two days after.

I ought to have recorded some times since, the Enemy's buffeting me at a prayer meeting. On the Thursday evening Mr. D. preached from these words, – 'Is Ephraim my dear son, is he a pleasant child, for since I spake against him, I do earnestly remember him still' etc. Ah, this was a sweet season, but at the prayer meeting next Lord's Day, he told me that the Lord had spoken against me, for that I was a cripple for life. At which I was so overcome that I could not look up. And then again, – he said, 'If you are called upon, how can you pray?'

Again I have been very remiss in not recording passages that were applied to my mind in my widowhood. At one time, this, –

'I know the thoughts that I think concerning you, thoughts of peace and not evil, to give you an expected end.'

At another, – 'Our God is the God of Salvation' etc., and in a time of temptation, – 'Because thou hast kept the word of my patience, I also will thee in the hour of temptation.'

O matchless goodness! Surely never did I see so much beauty and blessedness in these words as in my Widowhood, 'My Grace is sufficient for thee.'

June 18*th* 1846.
Mr. D. preached from 51 psalm, – 'Cast me not away from thy presence, and Take not thy Holy Spirit from me...' From this last date I went on very smoothly, within the means of grace. Very beneficial and for the most part mingled with enjoyment, and on the 7th November wak'd in the dawn of day, dreaming we walk by faith as strangers here, till Christ invites us home.

I thought I was standing under the gallery, and as I sung, I clapp'd my two hands together and as I did it, the young folks in the gallery opposite, seeing me do it, clapp'd their hands also, and the Clerk stair'd at me, – he also appreared to me a stranger.

1847. *January* 1. Again I would look back and record the goodness of God. . . . Blessed be to God for that support, and help yesterday, – in the morning these words, –

'Our days unheeded as they pass, and every swift revolving hour, are monuments of wondrous grace, and witness to his love and power.'

January 21. 47.
Between four and five this morning, had a most terrific dream. I thought I was somewhere in the country, and standing outside my friend's house I looked up to heaven and thought I see something like the funnell of a large steamer pointing down to the earth, and fire issuing out of the mouth thereof. As I turned into the house to tell my friends, it turned upwards and I awoke in a great humour, crying and shuddering.

May 19*th.*
At the church meeting this evening, I was, for the third time Nominated, with six others out of whom two were to be chosen as Deacons.

Mr. D. turned to Timothy's Epistle and made some very suitable remarks on what Deacons were called to do, and what they ought to be. The effect on me was very impressive, and humiliating.

I purposed in my mind not to go to any member's house during the month to say a word about it, not to bias anyone's mind.

On the following Friday morning, I was so overcome with the probability of being chosen, and feeling my weakness, I could not sing at family devotion. About this time, or the next day, when thinking of this business, the following words came to my mind, –

'The lot is cast into the lap but the whole disposing thereof is of the Lord.'

Oh, I thought, How calculated to quiet the mind if in
the minority. May I ever own Thy Hand.... Oh how
necessary is forbearance in the Church as well as in the
World.

June 16. 1847.
Church Meeting ... 'The Deacons' collected from pew to
pew, and those who had proxies had to take them to the
table pew, and when counted up, —

Belgrave had 123 and Warlow 110, leaving me in the
minority.

For which I was quite prepared, and was satisfied because
of my circumstances, and was glad it was over for it has
been a time of trial and temptation all the month.

Lords day. June 20. Mr. D. preached from the 85th Psalm, –
'Mercy and Truth have met together, righteousness and
peace have kissed each other ...' but I had such a barren
time I could not hear to profit.
In the evening he preached 33 Job, – 'Deliver him from
going down to jail for I have found a ransom' and among
other things he told us that some commentators said the
emphasis should be laid on the 'I have', – 'I HAVE found
a ransom' but what struck me most was the remarkable
coincidence between this discourse and a case visited by me
and by Brother Holiday this afternoon.
Which case was I requested to visit, in a friendly way,
by young Mr. Harvey. Did so, on May 31 the first time,

and on the following Lord's Day I got him on the Society, – and see him again the next week, besides taking Brother Thornton on June 13, and next week, twice again. Next Lord's day took Brother Holiday ... By all these visits the following things were developed, –

That he had been on a man of war, chief part of last war. That one time he was overboard between two and three hours when seven men had been dash'd off one of the yards, and he was the only person preserv'd. At another time, when sent ashore with a 24 pounder to storm some place, between 80 or 90 men were kill'd and he preserv'd, – all this led me to think he was a vessel of mercy, and led me to take other brethren to participate in the joy of seeing so aged a sinner return to God.

It appears that previous to my first visit, on the 31st May, he had been so distress'd on account of sin, that he was almost driven to despair, and was quite delerious at times.

His wife told Brother Wharton that all that had subsided after my first visit, and he acknowledg'd that I had been the means of leading him to Christ as a source of peace. On the following Wednesday he was very low, hardly able to speak, but did say, – 'Not my will but Thine be done' and express'd his confidence in Christ.

See him again on Saturday and he was so much better that he was sitting up in bed, reading an old book of prayers dedicated to the Prince of Orange a 100 years since.

June 20. *Lord's day*. Brother H. went with me, found him better and said he if he could possess all the world, he would not wish to fall back into a state of darkness and sin as before. We endeavour'd to encourage him in the hope of recovery, and he told me that some of his ancestors lived to be 110, but if so he was spared he hoped it might be to warn and instruct his children.

What made them objects of pity was his having 21 children, and 2 mishaps, and 7 of them born in 3 years. The man is 70, the wife 45 only.

June 23. See him again, asked him if he still felt as he did when he said he'd rather be as he was than possess all the world. His answer was 'yes', and he added that he was astonished that he had not seen these things before, that Christ was a Saviour in every way suited to us.

When I got downstairs, I found a room nearly full of children and relatives. Exhorted them all to seek the Lord. They listen'd and thank'd me for coming.

June 27. Brother Holiday and myself see him again found him patient and submissive. . . . And I said to him, 'This is the 4th visit but I have beg'd for you to have two more. Do you wish me to come, or some one else?' 'Oh no' he said, 'I hope you will come' and his wife also said they were glad to see me. . . . I found him happy in mind, and better in health.

July 21. See him again and he express'd himself as one firmly fixt on the rock of ages. In this month call'd upon to go to work. I went and was in attendance 6 days, – few hours, did 40, – and found myself too weak, therefore ask'd Mr. Hurcombe to excuse me altogether. But this was a trial, – for I had thought otherwise.

Sunday. October 18. Led to read the 58 Isaiah but so overcome, could not finish it. After prayer, had this sweet verse, – 'The promise of my Father's grace attend me all my days, nor from his house will I remove, nor cease to praise.'

1848. *March* 25. *Sunday.*
Mr. D. was led to speak from Jeremiah 33. verses 8 and 9. and after speaking of it literally, he spoke of it spiritually, and he said . . . the word 'iniquities' was derived from the root in the Hebrew which is 'perverseness', and the word 'transgress' in the Hebrew is 'obstinacy', – and I took more notice of the 9th verse, – 'and they shall fear and tremble' for that in the social meeting I could only hold up one hand to pray, – my trembling has been so much upon me, I have thought I should drop. I shall soon not be able to engage.

'Be gone unbelief, though creatures change.'

January 10*th.* 1849.
This morning, going to the workshouse to see one of our poor members, a man stopt me and told me I had been his Sunday School teacher, – 40 years ago, – and that he was a member of Milner's. Let God be glorified, no thanks to me, but the dear man thanked and blessed me again and again.

This winter I suffer more than ever in my hip. My pain and weakness is so that I cannot do as I would. But Glory be to God, He does all things well, – and every pain and woe I feel is but the fruit of sin.

January 31.
This is the third day I have been home, taking the Idra of Potash for the Rhuematics. Find myself very weak, but inclin'd to sing, – 'Let me but hear my Saviour say . . .'
Oh the mystery there is in our Afflictions, Here is one,

willing, by grace, to Visit the Afflicted but disabled by Affliction.

Yet shall not the Judge of all the Earth do right? 'Yes', I trust I can say, 'The Lord is my portion,' saith my soul, 'therefore will I hope in Him.'

I was full of heaviness yesterday morning. I fear it was my carnal mind produc'd it, – Lord save me from it.

When Josh (my son) lately came out of his time I trust my mind reclined on the Lord, – 'In everything by prayer and supplication make your requests known.'

June 13.

Had the misfortune to graze the skin off both my legs, which after having been plaster'd with white paper, by the Saturday following become so inflamed I had recourse to my old doctress and she applied her Ointment, – after dinner had a little sleep and waked with these words, – 'I would not change my bles'd estate, for all that Earth calls good and great . . .' with the very sweet remembrance of the indulgence I have the day before, riding with a friend to Acton, where at the Nunnery I see one of the Nuns walking in the Gardens with a black dress and a black veil. O how distressing to think of the bigotry of Catholicism. The scenery of the country was beautiful. But I was the subject of much pain and weakness.

August 24

For some time past, having suffer'd much pain night and day, and not being able to walk any distance, I was led to pray that God would lead me to the use of some means of relief, and I take it in answer and record it for the Glory of God, that I was led to a Shop close by the Bell foundry to buy some soap and linament and Spirits of Turpentine, and when I told the Doctor what it was for, – says he, – 'I will give you a bottle of Medicine which will do you no harm, if it does no good.' The which I took two doses before bedtime, and was surpris'd at the good effect, – but it was not lasting for when the first North wind came, my pains were as before.

Wednesday Sept. 5th.
Went to St. Jude's to hear Mr. Allen. Was much pleased and profited, got into conversation with his wife, and was recognised by their servant. Was very much struck with the Idea that much kindness from any friend produces the fear to offend, hence the Goodness of God leads to repentence.

1849. November 27.
Very frosty . . . much in pain, not out today. Reading in the life and times of Lady Hunt . . .n, I find that Mr. Nicholson went to Pell Street in the beginning of 1804, so that I have reason to believe that the Lord called me in my 17th year. But how many times have I vex'd and griev'd His Holy Spirit since then, – no wonder I am so afflict'd, but it is of the Lord's mercy that I am as I am. Oh for the grace to glorify Him, though it be in the furnace.

1850. January 2.
This morning was struck much with the goodness of God in having deliver'd me from the toils, the anxieties, cares and errors connected with the business and men of the World, these last ten years last August. Here also I would record His goodness in blessing the means of grace . . .

Through increasing weakness I am not able to attend the Infant School, as I was wont to do, – I very much regrett it, especially so as it is getting much into debt, and falling off, through a new teacher.

Feb'y 7th. This morning, about two o'clock, I was laying awake and these words was most sweetly brought to my mind, –

'HE careth for you'

Oh the sweetness and blessedness to know that the God of all Grace should care for such a poor sinner. How great is His goodness that endureth for ever.

April 30. *Whitsun.*
The last fortnight I was galvanised four times which cost 10/- but had no lasting effect. On this day when rising from secret prayer, it was as though some-one whisper'd into my left ear, – 'Nigh unto all them that call upon Me in truth'. Oh how encouraging, how blessed.

June 8th.
Have been to Chigwell and Loughton anniversaries within this last fortnight, had much enjoyment and reason for praise and thanksgiving. When I feel an inclination to fret and repine at my affliction, oh for an overcoming faith. 'Patience and strength, dear Lord afford. . .'

Lord's Day. November 17. '50.
Detain'd at home through a broken shin, done on the Tuesday before, trying to get into Darting's cart to go to prayer meeting. Trust I spent this evening to profit, reading in the Acts. Christiana also at home a fortnight.

D

27 *Nov*. Christiana so ill, forc'd to send for Doctor Hohry. My poor leg worse the last 3 days. Oh for patience and strength. 'Good Lord, subdue impatience and help me to rest on Thee...'

1851. *January* 1.
Another year of mercy, yet how far exceeding short I fall of what I ought to be. I am still so lame, such long nights, I get touchy, witless, and vex and perplexd and yet I have reason to say, 'Oh for an heart to praise my God', for blessed be to God, my Christiana is right well.

January 10
Our dear Pastor preached from Deuteronomy, – 'Boast not ye sons of Earth, nor look with scornfull eyes on the weeping Christian, for tears have their own sweetness.' I understand he was excellent.

April 24. This day I am 65. Oh what wondrous grace that I should be spared so long, having forfeited all claim to divine favour ... 47 years have rolled away since the Difference had been wrought, also what a many mercies I have receiv'd, how much patience and forbearance, long-suffering and goodness has been manifested, – and now that I enter my 66th year,

'Lord, continue to uphold and comfort me for thou knowest all my infirmities and relative burdens.'

May 25. So much pain, I went to Doctor Reeds in the evening ... Mr. D. overlook'd me in the morning and seeing me in so much pain, said what a good thing it would not be for ever...

He had been speaking from Romans 11th, last verse ... 'to whom be glory for ever.' It was good to be there, but I tremble so much.

July 2. Went to the Crystal Palace to see the wonderful works of God and of man. Truly I was animated in such a way that astonished those that were with me, myself also, – for I have had much pain lately, – I had thort I could not see it with pleasure.

Sept. 12*th*. Find myself weaker ... often am humbled under the mighty hand of God, and hoping for the time when I shall depart and be with Christ.

October. 19. With much pain went to Alice Street, enjoyed this means of grace and was much comforted with the Promise of my Father's grace...

October 30. Went to Founders Hall to give Notice that I wish to take up my livery by reason of the beadle having call'd for my quarterage, and giving me reason to hope I could do so. After many doubts and fears, and in hope to benefit my wife, I thought it my duty. When I arrived at the Hall I was usher'd into the presence of the clerk of the Comp..y who question'd and scrutinised me with much good feeling, and gave me to understand I need not expect it, but I could attend that day week, and the Court would consider, as it was their gift.

This left me without hope, and returning home this was my comfort and its force I felt, –

'Thank God. Be content with such things as ye have, for He hath said "I will never leave thee nor forsake thee." '

I afterwards consulted one of the Company, and thought it no use, nor did not go again, but gave it up. 1851.

1852. *July* 31.
Having been at Clapham four weeks, I have reason to record the great goodness of God, that through my dear friends Mr. and Mrs. Eddrup having a house furnish'd to let, we were honoured with the use of it, and might have stop'd longer but did not like to be absent two Ordinance days. While there, worship'd with the Independents at Mr. Duburg's Chapel in Park Cresent. My lameness and weakness induced me to go for the nearest, and my next door neighbour, – being a member there, was also a Visitor of the Samaritan Society which had been established about 30 years, – with him, I had communion, fellowship and trust. He was a dilligent visitor, for he told me he visited one for 24 successive weeks through want of another society near.

I went out while there, three times, – to a prayer meeting at the City Reform Almshouses in Shepherds Lane on Brixton Hill, and found it good to be there.

One evening, Monday, after our return from prayer meeting these words were very sweet, 'As thy days, so shall thy strength be.' I observe that it had been hotter that day than it had been known for years. It is true that I could not walk but went out for an hour now and then in an Invalid Chair at 1/3 per hour and 1/- to a friend's house and 1/- back, – but in this I found long enough for Cramp.

We had a very pleasant day the day before we came home and rode in an open carriage and with two horses round Streatham Common, past Beulah Spa and the place they were clearing for the Crystal Palace and through Sydenham. Was much pleased with the views and scenery, – Oats standing in Sheaf, – new buildings. Stop't at Dartmouth Arms to turn from there over Forrest Hill, Peckham Rye, Peckham, Camberwell, Cole Harbor Lane, Brixton Tulse Hill and across to Streatham place to tea at Mr. Eddrup's after which came the Invalid Chair to fetch me home. We spent a delightfull day. Mr. Eddrup call'd at Peckham to give a pensioner of his 13/ ag^{rs} money.

Shame and confusion of face belongs to me that I should let so much of the year pass, and not to notice the abounding goodness already manifested to me.

Why I am this day more out of debt than I have been for the last seven or eight years, besides the manifestation of God's presence giving me relief from pain. . .

Had a good day yesterday and blessed be to God, one of my first thoughts this morning was, – 'God with us.'

October. 19.
This morning and yesterday while lying awake the last verse of a hymn was brought to my mind with such sweetness that I was astonished and especially so when I found it was a hymn we were not in the habit of singing. After some search found it by means of the Index, – 'Jesus, how glorious is thy grace, When in thy Name we trust. . .'

Nov. 9.
About one or two this morning I was awaked with pain and trembling, and if I mov'd or tried to turn, it put me in fresh pain, – besides which when I thought of the houses and their getting out of repair, and then again, if anyone was Killed, and I should be tried for Manslaughter, what a

disgrace, and what a Reproach, – then I had such a trembling come over me that I could not rest in my bed, and was in and out of my bed six times. Drew a light, burnt it out, lit another and then thought it would help keep me awake, then put it out. . . After a little while as I lay, I knew that the wall had been look'd to, and that I had given orders for it to be pull'd down, but the man did what he thought enough. I trembled again, till at length it occur'd to my mind, –

'On Me depend, I'm Jesus still, the sinner's
Friend. Thou need'st not be afraid.', –

after which my fear and trembling ceas'd and I got into a sweet sleep. Bless'd be to God.

The same words had been much bless'd to me eight or nine years ago.

1853. *June* 11.
I have been very remiss lately in not writing, but I can only account for it through want of disposition and having nothing worth Notice. I go on from day to day and have reason to say, – 'My rising and my setting sun rolls gently up and down the hill.' Many days last month afraid to go out, because of the prevailing NE winds. I got out one day, went only round one street and home again. The weather has been finer this month, blessed be to God.

But such is our weakness and pain that we have been readdy to weep over each other. Sometimes I have been inclined to say 'Let me lay down and die, – and go out no more.' However the Lord has helped me and led me to Dr. Reid's, on a week night evening, – and I have found it good to be there. Ah, last night week, after two brethren had engaged in prayer the Dr. made some remarks on that passage in the closing part of St. Jude. 'Presented faultless before His Glory...' Oh, the word 'presented' and whereas I had been reading the same day in the Newspaper respecting the great and many that were presented before the Queen at her Drawing room, and then in my mind I contrasted the one with the other, and oh the vast difference, – and how many may be presented before the Queen that give little or no evidence that they will ever be presented before the King of Kings.

The following Friday after two had prayed, Dr. Reid gave us a few thoughts on these words, –

'Without Me ye can do nothing'

That, we all experimentally knew the truth of that saying, especially in approaching the Throne of Grace, and though it might seem discouraging at times, we might find the answer in his Word to the Apostle, – 'My grace is sufficient for thee.' and in like manner to every believer. Thus I discover it is good to wait on the Lord, though it be not among those of our own denomination, –

Good God forgive our narrow mindedness.

1853. *August* 24.
Since I last wrote, me Wife Christiana and I have been four weeks to Mitcham, but deriv'd no benefit. Was often inclin'd to sing, – 'Father whate'er of Earthly Bliss...' etc. but we did it for the best, in hope that a change of Air would be at once beneficial.

Was too far from a place of worship, – could not go for a ride, but both of us was lifted in and out of the cart. Would not go to Ramsgate because of our weak and helpless state, and being forc'd to have one of our daughters with us. After four weeks was glad to get home, – the worse than when we went.

Alas, the return of this month reminds me, on the 11th August '39, fourteen years ago, I bruis'd my hip joint. Lately I have been much exercised with pain that I find it quite enough to go to Doctor Reid's and, blessed be to God, find it good to be there.

Oh what a mercy to feel the mind at liberty to worship with any of God's people.

Still, I must say, no place like home, – though sometime I was inclined to say 'neglected, despised and forgotten, no man careth for my soul,' yet I know it is written, – 'He careth for you.'

Again, – 'He despiseth not the prayer of the destitute.' Or as the Poet says 'His ear attends the softest call, His eyes can never sleep. . .' how many times have I prov'd the truth of this when sleepless I have lain, and when in pain how I have been led to see that He has power over both soul and body. Oh what a mighty Saviour we have to do with.

'Bless the Lord Oh my soul, and all that is within me bless His Holy Name.'

Appendix

By his son, William Swan, –

'My dear father was born on April 24, 1786. At the age of nineteen it pleased God to call him, by His Grace, and tho' his parents were unkind to him on that account, he went to work as a journeyman bricklayer at the building of the London Docks.

Afterwards through the kindness of friends he became a Citizen and Fellowship porter, and God also gave him favour in the sight of Mr. Saunders through whose interest he became Deputy Corn Meter.

Having married at the age of twenty-one, he worked hard, – and affectionately brought up a family of ten children, – except one who died at six years, – He was an industrious, practical Christian, energetic and faithful to his profession.

At the close of his life he suffered much bodily affliction, but he patiently endured until March 8th. 1854, – he peacefully resigned his spirit.

Buried at Bow Cemetery, Bow Road, London.'

The Journal of
WILLIAM SWAN

born 1813

'I will sing of mercy and judgment; unto thee O Lord, will I sing.'

The writer was born May 17th 1813, at Lower Cornwall Street, St. George in the east, London, of godly, affectionate and industrious parents. For my Father and Mother feared God, above many, – this is a great mercy and privilege. For I can truly say, – 'I was my Father's son, tender and only beloved in the sight of my Mother.'

Not that they made a favourite of me. . . There were ten in family and I was the third child and the first son. I can remember my Mother often speaking of one of my sisters, who while carrying me downstairs at an old-fashioned house in the City, let me slip from her arm over her shoulder, by which falling in the corner of the stairs I was very much hurt, so that I remained with my neck bent for a long time.

When I was very young, my Father used to carry me with him on Sunday mornings, to Little Alice Street Baptist Chapel, – he being a member there. After this, when I was about seven years of age, my Father removed to Philip Street, St. Georges.

Herein was contained much of the goodness of God to

myself, and all the family, – it being the constant care of our parents to feed and clothe and instruct us. Although my Father worked hard, rising early and labouring hard, yet he found time to instruct and correct his family when necessary. About this time my two elder sisters, myself, and the next brother, attended Sunday School at Rev. Andrew Reed's Chapel, Cannon Street Road, – also I was sent to a day school.

After a while myself and brother Thomas were recieved into the Stepney Meeting House Free School but we did not remain there more than two years, – Father's employment becoming more lucrative he took us away from the free school, and the Committee very much applauded his integrity.

There was a good master at that school, whose habit it was to talk to the boys in a very solemn and becoming manner, and I well remember many of his words of truth and council, warning and caution, spoken at proper times. And many dear hymns we sung. While at that school we attended Sunday mornings at Stepney Meeting House, Dr. Josh Fletcher being the Pastor.

After this, I and Thomas were sent to paid school again until we were more than 13 years of age, and I have often wished that the teaching of those days had been up to the standard of the present day.

It pleased God to give me very serious thoughts of myself as a sinner before God, and being unfit to die, so that in this early part of my boyhood I felt very much concern about my immortal soul. I felt a persuation in my own mind that those who feared God in this world were the happiest of men and women, and had the best hope of and prospect of, an eternal state.

My Father, being a man of prayer, always gathered his

family in the evening to read the Scriptures to us, and after that always prayed aloud very fervently for our spiritual welfare, not forgetting temporal matters at the same time, – so that by prayer and thanksgiving in all things he made known his requests to God.

In these days, in the prime of his life, I think he was one of the most happy and cheerful men in the world. So punctual in attending the house of God on Sundays, and week evenings when possible. Being thus kindly trained and tutored I attended Alice Street Chapel under the ministry of Mr. Shenston.

When getting toward the age of 13 I got something to do between school hours, after that an errand boy's place at an Ironmonger and Tinman shop. Meanwhile Father intended to bind me apprentice to some business. Having been so cared for and nurtured at home, I, at first, felt it very hard to go out into the world, not being used to rough language or treatment, and for a boy I had not much courage.

As I got near 14, a Mr. Kemp advised Father to get me, on liking, to Mr. Volkman, Confectioner, of Stratford Essex, with a view to apprenticeship. In the month of May, 1827, according to agreement, my Father took me to Mr. Volkman. After being a few weeks on trial, I was bound to serve seven years as an indoor apprentice to learn the business. But oh what a change I found it to be! Having been so kindly treated at home and then to go among strange men and five or six fellow apprentices, and no one to speak a kind word to me. Also the long day's work required, – often working until nine and ten at night, and at the shortest from six in the morning until eight o'clock at night. The effect of all which was to make me very desponding in mind.

After about six months had elapsed I was taken badly of rheumatism and obliged to go home to my Father. There I remained laid up of rheumatic fever for seven weeks at the end of which I returned to Stratford.

But I was much grieved, because neither the master nor one of the sons spoke a word to me, or said, 'Well Bil., glad to see you back. . .'

Now for the first three years of my time I was kept at drudgery and dirty work, so that nearly half of the seven years passed away before I was put to work at the trade to fit me to get employment.

My master, although a Wesleyan, was always driving-on at business, and I can safely say, although I was an indoor apprentice, I never saw a Bible in his hand.

Whether from the damp atmosphere, or depression of spirits, or both, about the age of seventeen I became subject to Asthma of the lungs. My chief comfort at this time was to get home early on Sunday mornings to go to Alice Street Chapel, – which my Mother encouraged me in. I have often walked up the Commercial Road without breakfast to get to Chapel.

However this did not long escape the notice and derision of the other apprentices. . .

(I should have said that my Mother always got a good breakfast at home for me.)

Up to 1830 I had not made much progress at learning to fit me for a journeyman, and other apprentices coming after me, especially one called Stevens, – got some advantage over me. I was very timid and shy, and also sly, – for this I must confess, to my shame.

But about this time it pleased God, – for I trust that it was the gracious work of God, the Eternal Spirit, to shew me somewhat of my state as a sinner before God. This was chiefly under the ministry of Mr. Shenston at Little Alice Street.

Now surrounded as I was, and having no one to talk to during the week, – nor having any place or private bedroom to retire to from the company of others, and no opportunity to pray alone, nor leisure to read, – yet God, albeit, often blessed the word of truth and grace to my soul, such a passage (remembered) as this, –

'I will have mercy, and not sacrifice, for I am not come to call the righteous, but sinners to repentence', and many texts of Scripture spoken from Sabbath to Sabbath.

Also, on Sunday afternoons, I used to go to Cumberland Street, Curtain Road, to hear Dr. Andrews of Walworth preach. He was a very eloquent and faithful preacher. How I used to admire that dear man! How I used to wish I could speak to him! Many texts he spoke from, and parts of his sermons remained, and are sometimes present, in my mind. Also Joseph Irons, Henry Heap and Doctor Collyer I would hear when they came into the City on Sabbath afternoons.

At all this dear Father and Mother were very much pleased – (I had a dear loving Mother) – and at times I thought myself very good, but soon I got into a despairing state of mind again, through guilt. I have been guilty of swearing with my fellow apprentices and also worrying and teazing a poor half-idiot in the master's employ. To my shame I recollect this. He was a harmless hard-working man getting on in years.

Having served about half of my seven years I began to get a little more forward with the work, and as was the custom, I was paid 3d per hour overtime after fourteen hours per day. After a while my master set me to another part of the work which was considered superior, – the making of almond cakes etc. –

This overtime pay, small as it was, was some help, for my Father was not able to get me all the clothes I needed, having so many in family, and my board and lodging and that pay was all I was paid during the whole seven years apprenticeship.

In 1832 I became more affected with Asthma of the lungs and was laid up about seven weeks, and attended an Infirmary in Spitalfields under Doctors Davis and Ramadge. I was twice bled and blistered on the chest, and with the treatment and care I recovered more strength and returned to work.

At that time I felt much despondency of mind and some persons considered that I was Consumptive. I had many gloomy thoughts and feelings, but I was favoured with some hope in the mercy of God.

Some time before this, in consequence of my saying some saucy words to an elderly man, he instantly, – being at work at the oven, – in the most spiteful and cruel manner let the long handle or shaft of the peel fall with great violence on the crown of my head. It was a great mercy that it did not break the skull, but the Lord prevented me from further injury than the sharp blow at the time.

But thus I was placed among a deal of strife and nothing thought of by the master but work, work. . . .

Now it happened in 1832, during June, that I was at home from illness, that there was two doors off my Father's, then living with her Aunt, a very lively and cheerful young woman, and I heard my Father speak some words of commendation concerning her to my Mother. Such was Harriet Glass, the picture of health and cleanliness.

We became acquainted. On my part, it was for the sake of company.

As to the workshop, it was not a very comfortable one, inasmuch that the master did not care who he employed, respectable or otherwise, or about the example he set before apprentices. As to myself, tho I continued to attend Chapel on Sundays I had not the courage to be decided in the service of God.

To my shame I confess I indulged in the sin of swearing at times. Thus I went on, sinning and repenting, and felt a bondage of mind because of my sins. My dear Father would often give me some good words of counsel and advice, also my Mother's affection was not at all abated.

June 1833. In consequence of two journeymen leaving the employ, I was sent to work at the master's shop in the City, and at best work chiefly, and there in the last year in seven I worked very hard. The workshop being in a cellar in Bishopsgate Street was very dark and unhealthy.

At length, the term being completed, I was set on, as a journeyman, and my work gave satisfaction. When I came out of my time, I was very much in want of clothes.

Now altho I had served seven years to learn the business, yet I had a good deal more need of practice, the aim of the master being chiefly to get hands to do some of his work. Whether from want of genius on my part or otherwise, I was not as proficient as I should have been, neither was I competent to take the work at many single-handed places in the line.

From the time I came to the City I had many more opportunities to see my sweetheart, and so it was that we became very fond, but as yet I had not been able to earn the money to make a home.

After six months had passed away, I being the object of dislike to a bad man, the foreman at Volkman's City shop, – I left. It was as well I did leave for it was an unwholesome cellar to work in, and by gaslight.

Through the help of a fellow workman, the next job I had was three months at Kilner's, Hanway Street, Oxford Street. But during this first year after I was out of my time, we, that is myself and my Harriet, who was to be my wife, done very foolishly.

We became too familiar . . . ah, this brought guilt into my conscience indeed, and my companion was, by our folly, brought into trouble.

1835.

In the Spring, I was taken on at Stratford, – as a journeyman, of course. I then soon, by the advice of my Father, and from his copy, took up the Freedom of the City of London, and also the Fellowship, which cost me upwards of £12. (£5 for the fellowship only.)

In this year, my Father's Mother died, from the effects of a fall, at the age of 72.

My companion, having left her aunt, Mrs. King, and gone to her Father's because of her condition, in December, gave birth to a fine girl. (Mrs. King did not shew kindness to her niece, tho she had worked well for her aunt, and had kept her house like a little palace.)

I stayed at work at Stratford until 1836. In the autumn I left, of my own account, to go to Haslams, Bethnal Green Road, but there I was not suited to the work. Next (after 4 months) I had three months again at Hanway St. Oxford Street. During this time I lodged as much as I could at my Father's house.

E

1837. I suffered much distress of mind because of my folly, and because of the trouble and disgrace brought upon my companion, yet I did see it was duty to marry, which it certainly was. I used to think there could be no mercy for me. 'I have sinned against light and knowledge.'

In June I applied to Mr. Volkman, at Stoke Newington, he having begun business there three years ago. So I went to work there, the same year in which Queen Victoria came to the throne. Here was a large and airy bakehouse in an healthy locality, and in the goodness of God I was prospered in my work, and esteemed for it. Employed here during three years from 1837, and more comfortable than I had been.

In 1838 I was married at St. John. of Hackney to Harriet Glass. Now I had not much to make a home with in money for what with a decent stock of clothes, and taking up my freedom upon moderate wages, and paying to the support of my child, I was not permitted to be a waster. . . . However I felt it my duty to marry and I thank God that I felt pleasure in so doing.

Before the year's end my partner gave birth to a little girl, at about seven months, thro a fright, but it died the next day.

1839. From the time that I began to keep house the Lord enabled me to observe the Sabbath day and also to read some portion of the word of God every evening, also in my feeble manner to pray with my wife and children when the family increased. I was advised to do so by a good man of the name of Deane, a Deacon of Alice Street Chapel, whom I respected, having known him for years. To him I was able to open my mind when in trouble, and as a dear Christian friend he councelled and advised me.

When living in Union Street, Stoke Newington I attended the Ministry of Mr. Curtis, Homerton, an affectionate and faithful preacher, to my mind.

But I still continued in much darkness of unbelief, because of the guilt of my sins and my ignorance of salvation. Yet it pleased God to bless some portions of his holy word to my soul.

My dear wife seemed happy and comfortable now.

1840. I continued to work at Stoke Newington, and in the Spring the work increased so that we were kept at very long hours. I fell into the snare of being the first to complain to the master, while my fellow workers left me to do the best I could, and as the master and I got to rather high words about the long hours, – I had warning to leave.

In July, I left the work at Stoke Newington, not feeling disposed to beg pardon, and with a very sad heart I was again called to seek employment. The next job offered was work at Mr. Nuthalls at Kingston in Surrey. I used to walk the 16 miles from Newington on Sunday evenings, lodge and board in the house and return home on Saturday nights. But oh! How different the work, and having to work again in a cellar, – in the very hot July and August, it was a small and stinking cellar, tho in a country town. Add to this the grief of mind on account of having lost the work at Newington in an unguarded manner...

Altogether, at the end of eight weeks I was laid with spitting of blood which rendered me unable to work for the following six weeks.

At the end of this time, being but poorly from my illness, and my health not very robust from the long confinement of the work, I walked up to the City, day by day, for a while to seek work as a Fellowship porter, and got employ, more or less. My health improving, about the beginning of 1841, we removed to Richard Street, Commercial Road, E. London.

I continued at this work, laboured at the waterside as a Fellowship porter, and on board ship, such as working corn out of vessels or backing potatoes, corn, malt, salt or coals, oysters and mussels, – anything I could get to do, and had a good share of health, thank God.

In April my first son was born, and as in other times so with this, my William, his Mother had a very favourable time through the goodness of God, and our daily wants were supplied.

In this way the change done myself and my family good. During this time I attended Alice Street Chapel, chiefly, and often the Lord was pleased to bless the word to my support. Having many cares and anxieties, for there was more care required to get work then, I did in fact find that God often directed my steps.

1842. Followed on at the same work, with my partner and our three little ones in good health, through the goodness of God. I was enabled to bear the changes of weather and seasons, altho I had been used to indoor work prior to this.

About this time, Mrs. Swan's Aunt, Mrs. King, died, and about the middle of the year we removed to take a house in Jane St., Commercial Road, at 18 guineas a year, taking the Joyces for lodgers in the best apartments and living in the kitchen ourselves. But herein I found myself soon embarrassed for the Joyces failed to pay, and also the next lodgers, Paxton by name, a boot maker whom I had known years before, – but he had become idle and a drunkard, – not knowing this when I took them. So I suffered loss, and had often to work to pay their rent as well as ours.

Afterwards let the rooms to J. Barrow, a porter with myself, but it was with difficulty that I got his money.

1843. In March my former master at Stratford sent for me to come to work, which I did on the next Monday, 20th, and during that first week I had an opportunity to go home, – and so was able to fetch the doctor to my wife who had a fine boy, we called Richard. Again my wife recovered nicely and was able to go out within a month.

My work at Stratford only lasted six weeks, and Good Friday occured during that. They thought they had too many men so I had to leave. However, it was a help to us as the other work was very slack at the time.

While living in Jane Street, the girls, Harriet and Margaret, came in from school one morning and Margaret being pleased with an orange her school mistress had given her, ran to show it to her Mother when she slipped and put the right hip bone out of joint, – for so it terminated. Altho we had the doctor and took her to the London Hospital, the injury could not be recovered and she became lame.

Thus I went on, sometimes at one sort of work, at times at something else ... B. Baker, of Shoreditch came, and asked me to come to work for him at my trade which I did, part-time, as that was all he wanted.

In all, what with an increasing family, and uncertain work, and a hard man for my Landlord so that I often had to pay rents whether I got my lodgers money or not, I became scarcely able to keep decent clothes to go to Chapel in. So I went sometimes to Mr. Milners at Pell Street, or elsewhere.

I bless God, He has often blessed the sermons to my soul's comfort and support. Under distress and toils and discomfort at home, it is a mercy to be kept seeking the Lord.

1843.

In the early part of October, Mr. Volkman sent for me to come to work part-time. So I went, making up my time out of doors.

I should have written that in May my dear Mother died, very happy in the Lord, after 18 months of debility. My father was laid aside with lameness of the hip, but he had a salary of £60 a year from his pension fund, and the rental of a few houses.

Thus the time passed on, – I being sometimes at Newington, and the remainder at the Waterside, where, with a good deal of toil and running about for it, together with the uncertainty of the work, we found it difficult to get enough for ourselves and the children and also to pay the rent. . .

1844. I think it was in the early part of this year that the Landlord, as I had got into arrears with the rent, even to £5, determined to get us out of the house, and when I returned home one evening, I found the Broker's man in. Now came the difficulty, – how to save my goods? But again the Lord appeared for us, – in my distress I went to Stoke Newington and Mr. V. lent me £1-5-0 which I paid afterward at 5/- a week, and what with selling a chest of drawers etc. in all made up about half the amount, and the Landlord let us go. So through the kind help of Mr. Volkman, and by Little, the Landlord, being disposed to let me go, by getting a part, – we removed to a court in Batty Street, Commercial Road.

From this, I was kept on chiefly at Stoke Newington, and as they were short handed we were kept at work late, even until ten and ten thirty from six in the morning, so that I walked home to Com'l Road three or four nights each week, to save paying for lodgings. This continued through the winter of '44 and so into a new year.

1845. By this time, Mrs. Swan was again expecting to be a Mother, which made me very anxious, working so far from home. I returned on the night of February 27 and about three next morning my dear wife was safely delivered of twin children, a boy and girl, prematurely, tho about 7 months. An old friend of my father's, a Miss Rayment being very kind to my partner, I had a nurse to attend to Mrs. Swan and the children, but she most shamefully neglected both mother and children.

It was a mercy that it did not result in permanent injury to Mrs. Swan which it very probably would have done, but for the kindness of her sister, Charlotte, who came from Lewisham on a visit to see her, about the ninth or tenth day of her confinement, and seeing how neglected a condition she was in, – set to, in a most kind and motherly manner, and attended to Mrs. Swan and the children, getting them what changes etc. were required in the best way she could.

Here was proof of the affection of her sister Charlotte, and the interposition of the providence of God for us.

Now having six children, and the eldest but just turned nine years, myself away at Newington and that long hours,

I was glad to earn what money I could tho badly paid, but more, – this worthless nurse robbed us and also robbed us of coals for which we had to pay 2/6 per cwt at that time, – besides there set in from the day of my wife's confinement four weeks of intense cold weather, frost, severe, heavy falls of snow, Russian like weather which lasted 28 days, such as I have never known to the present.

Well, in the course of four or five weeks, with the blessing of God, my partner regained more strength, and I was continuing at Stoke Newington in work, – we therefore desired to move to Newington which we did, in July 45, taking a small house in Brook Street, Clapton, at £1 per month, of Mr. Burton, – with a small garden in front and a nice piece behind, in an healthy situation. We soon all felt the benefit of. . .

My Margaret, then not six years old, had been attending the London Hospital for the lameness of her hip, and was now only able to get about on crutches, but she soon benefitted from the change.

The dear little twins had been sickly from birth, – it so happened that the boy, we named him Joseph, died of convulsions on the morning of the Thursday following our removal from town, and was buried at Old Hackney Churchyard.

But withal there was much cause for thankfulness, – myself at work, and with a good prospect of it, after the toils and uncertainties and reverses, altho sometime with a good measure of success and at times but with just strength enough and none to spare. . . . In fact, I was not strong enough for some of the outdoor work, yet to be out in the air done good to my health, but at my business there was less anxiety.

So we benefitted from the change and from that time I attended Homerton Row Chapel, and the Lord was most graciously pleased to bless to my soul the ministry of His Word, under Mr. Daniel Curtis, – in many texts and sermons, and in the friendship and conversation of some neighbours and members with whom I walked there and back frequently. Which again, gave me more hope and encouragement in the grace of God, – for indeed, I had been a long time struggling with besetting sins and doubts and fears, and the common adversary took great advantage of my state of mind. It is a great mercy that I feel able to write down these things now which transpired many years ago, and some of them appear quite fresh to my mind – with the help of the few notes I have by me written when I had time.

1846. Early in this year, I was persuaded by my wife's entreaty to give Mrs. Lawson, her sister, a lodging with us, she being in want, and forsaken of her husband, if she could get some work near at hand. But her conduct never proved very commendable, and about this time, tho without my consent, Mrs. Swan would go out to work, at Washing and Ironing, – at both of which she was expert.

I endeavoured to persuade my wife otherwise, feeling sure a wife can do best her duty at home, – to which she would not agree, – but alas! . . . in going out there was a sad habit acquired of taking strong drink. . .

1847.
Now tho changes had taken place at the shop, the business increased, and with the measure of health and continued

employ, we were enabled to feed the children. Sometimes friends and neighbours gave little articles of clothing, and so did Mrs. Swan's sister, Charlotte.

Having by this time attended a good while at Homerton Row, and conversed very freely with the friends there, the Lord in his rich grace and free love and merciful teachings continued to bless my soul, – and yet I remained ignorant of the way of Salvation. Many precious texts and sermons had been sweetly blest to my soul's comfort, such as 'He restoreth my soul', Psalm 23.

Well one day as I was much perplexed in mind, with this thought, – 'How can a man be just with God?' (and I was at my work) I trust that it was Jehovah the Eternal Spirit, applied this to my mind, – 'Behold my servant whom I uphold; mine elect in whom my soul delighteth' ... Isaiah Chapter 42. verse 1 ... giving me to see that Christ condescended to become God's servant and thus also became God's way of salvation for man. Of what a sweet time of happy deliverance to my soul thus to hope, in God, for the forgiveness of sins through his own appointed way of salvation even Jesus Christ. For truly I had been in bondage nearly seventeen years but this was the Lord's time, a time of Love. Thanks be to God.

Now as the time passed on so cheerfully with the Lord's presence, I desired the communion and fellowship of the people of God, – but I thought myself unworthy of notice. At length, about one Sunday in June, Mr. Curtis took his text from Ezra, Chapter 9 verse 8, — 'And now for a little space, grace hath been shewed from the Lord our God.' At the close of the service I was emboldened to speak to Mr. Curtis, who kindly said, 'Come and see me tomorrow evening' ... in the most affectionate manner he received and heard me, and afterwards proposed me to the Church for membership.

I waited until September, when no others coming forward, I was baptised alone. My dear Father, then about 62, but infirm with his hip, and my brother Joseph, came to tea with me, and to hear the sermon and see the Ordinance administered. Mr. Curtis preached, from Peter, and my Father who was now old in the ways of the Lord, said that he had never heard a better baptismal sermon.

It was indeed a happy season, as was the following Sabbath when I was publicly admitted into the Church of Christ. October 3, '47.

Our dear Pastor said, 'You know something of the conflict, brother, but the Lord is well pleased for His Righteousness Sake. . .'

Blessed be to God, my mind has not lost all the sweet remembrance of it, and from that time the Lord led me on cheerfully.

In July my partner presented me with another son, a fine big boy he was when born, to whom we gave the name of Philip. Thus making our family six in number and the parents made eight, in all. The Lord supplied our temporal wants.

. . . In the good providence of God I was kept at work and with overtime. The children and my wife enjoyed a good measure of health and we all enjoyed returning Sabbaths. As the young grew they attended the Sunday School at Clapton Chapel where they recieved good instruction. Mrs. Swan continued to take some washing in . . . (But small houses are not suited to laundry work and a family to live in . . .)

Towards the close of '49 my wife's Uncle C. Glass died,

by which after affairs were settled my wife was to receive a small legacy of £10, – but it did not come to hand until a year.

1850.

As I had been for some weeks so I continued in the early part of this year to suffer from rheumatism and debility for which I attended the Dispensary under Dr. Seive King who gave me Cod Liver Oil to take during thirteen weeks, – but with little benefit to my health.

Yet I was enabled with just enough strength to keep at work. Whether the close confinement of my work or anxiety were the most hurtful I cannot say. When June 20th arrived Mrs. Swan recieved the £10 from her Uncle's legacy, and this was an anxiety, – but as it happened we were both at work and some washing in the house, so time was not found to spend it directly. We had thought of doing so chiefly in clothes, bedding and necessaries, – but there was another path to tread and for myself the path of affliction, – yet the Lord supported and brought us through it.

Just a week after my wife had this money, I was taken at work spitting of blood, so I was obliged to leave off. This continued and produced great weakness. In the evening, the most violent attack occured, I brought up a large quantity of blood which resulted in complete prostration. My wife, much alarmed, paid every attention she could, going to the Dispensary, etc. but the doctor said he could do no more for me. Upon this, some ice was got and laid upon my chest, which no doubt had a good effect.

It had so happened my friend and fellow member came in to see us, (John Brown, the gardener) and after fetching

Mr. Rainbow to see me, – and they not knowing of my illness before this, – were much affected and John Brown sat up with me all night, considering I was in a very dangerous condition. I have much reason to record the goodness of God under this affliction.

My mind was much comforted by many passages of scripture and verses of hymns, altho my body was reduced to the weakness of a child for about 10 days. Yet after nearly four weeks I began to amend, and even during that time I had been able to take some food.

Christian friends, and Mr. Curtis were very kind, and even some neighbours, to come in to enquire, and see me.

Now as I began to take more food I was subject to constipation of the bowels on account of which Mrs. S. called in a Mr. Fliescher, Homeopathic doctor and I obtained relief, – at which, when the doctor of the dispensary heard, he walked away. The fact was those doctors were glad to get rid of my case, for they had said I could not get up again, that one lung had gone, – but it pleased God to raise me up again.

'The gates of the devouring grave are open'd wide in vain.'

The Lord supplied our wants. Altho a neighbour had got the washing away which Mrs. Swan had had for sometime and which came to £3 per week, yet during the illness my master gave us towards our supply, £3. 10. and Christian friends were very kind with their gifts, and it was beautiful weather, so that the air helped to do me good so that by the middle of September I went back to work. Altho weak, my master wanted to see me back, – yet I felt more or less of the weakness during three years.

I should note that during the last six weeks of the time I was recovering, chiefly out in the air, I was not overtaken by rain or storm while walking or riding, so that I had the full benefit of fine weather, – through the goodness of God.

1851.
In March we came under new rules, that of men going home to board. Whereas formerly journeymen had boarded in the Master's house during the six working days, – the change being more comfortable for men and their families. About this time we got Harriet a place of servitude, and the boys to the Lancasterian School.

1853.
Lost my brother Joseph, only 22 years of age, by drowning in the London Docks, which was a grief to all but more especially to my Father for he suffered much.

About the middle of the year Mr. Curtis after some month's illness, departed this life, after more than sixteen years pastorate. At first there were various supplies but soon came Mr. William Palmer, and after about six months he accepted the pastorate, – a faithful affectionate preacher, profound in thought, clear in expression and firm in the truth and consistant . . . he continued until his removal by death in 1873.

In November '53 my Father was confined to his room, this being his last illness, he never came downstairs again. Sunday after Sunday I used to go to see him to give him company and tell him as much as I could remember of the sermon in the morning by Mr. Palmer which was always cheering to his spirits. Then he was subject to despondancy and very much worried by the common adversary of souls, – but His heavenly Father was about to take him home. Truly he suffered much bodily affliction, but with great patience and submission to the will of God. Also his wife was the subject of a very painful disorder and confined to the bedroom and unable to help, – very grievous.

1854. Thus my father continued, and I saw him each Sunday when we sang and prayed and talked together until March 8th when he peacefully resigned his spirit, – and I doubt not that his Saviour whom through grace he had long loved and served, recieved him into his ever lasting kingdom. His remains were buried in Bow Cemetary, Bow Road, London, – just a twelvemonth after the death of my young brother Joseph.

The males of the family and Mr. Dickerson, Mr. Belgrave, Mr. Wharton and others following . . . and Mr. Dickerson officiating at the Chapel and the graveside. The next Sabbath evening Mr. Dickerson spoke from Psalm 37 verses 39 and 40, – 'But the salvation of the righteous is of the Lord, he is their strength in the time of trouble.

And the Lord shall help them; he shall deliver them from the wicked and save them, because they trust in him.'

Mr. Palmer, not knowing of my loss, took for his text in the morning, Psalm 37, verse 18, – 'The Lord knoweth the days of the upright and their inheritance shall be for ever . . .'

About this time, our youngest son, Philip suffered from weakness of the right ancle, he having had rheumatic fever, for which we took him to the Orthopaedic Institution, Soho, where he was operated on, and the foot placed in a kind of frame, and afterward he had a boot with irons up the leg, fastened with straps. He bid fair to get straight on the foot, but from the weakness or from too much use of the foot, the operation had to be repeated. Even then, he being an active boy, would go too much on the foot, in consequence we failed. I was kept close at my work to get our bread, but I did think those at home to blame, for Mrs. Lawson was with us a good deal of this time.

Towards the end of the year I had to go to seek out-door work again, being slack at the shop and my Master using me very unfairly in that he put all lost time upon me, thus making a convenience of me, – not that there was any blame due to my work that I can truly say, – thank God. But this was a cross he was permitted by God to lay on me, permitted by my Heavenly Father – and often my health improved by the change and more money earned... altho I could not have home comforts.

Now my lads began to get little places between school hours which was helping to us, and they made good progress at Sunday and day school, – as to my daughters I was never able to give them so much schooling as I wished, – they were regular at Sunday school. And these were among the happiest days of my fleeting life, when the children gathered round and we sung and conversed and sometimes prayed with them. Peaceful happy Sabbaths we had, and the Lord placed us in good providence.

It was a healthy locality to bring up a family in, and myself the walk to and fro Homerton Row and spending the Sabbath aright did so refresh both body and mind that I often felt quite young again on Mondays.

And the Lord continued to bless to my soul words of truth and grace by the ministry of Mr. Palmer whose sermons were instructing and edifying and also had a practical bearing.

1855.

Thus we continued. I was at the shop for some months and then out of doors to work, and the lads one or both at work at Laws Nursery Clapton, and after that Richard worked at Mrs. Ford's, – Cowkeeper. Mrs. Swan would go out somedays to ironing, altho I never consented to it. Also her health and strength began to fail, – possibly the malady then commenced by which she eventually fell.

I think it was before the close of '56, being in want of work, I applied at Stratford and was taken on, so I was again obliged to be away from home all the week and this continued during 1857. Mrs. Swan was very dissatisfied at my absence from home which I could not avoid, however she was very weakly and there was not that order kept in the house there should have been. During the summer all the family except Margaret, myself and Mrs. Swan, suffered from scarlet or typhus fever which induced much weakness in Martha and required time for recovery. Harriet was near getting married, but being siezed with the fever it was hindered. Mrs. Swan was now suffering from abcess of the stomach and alas was very impatient.

1858.

As I had to leave home on Sunday evenings to go to Stratford to lodge, to be in for work on Monday morns, it being winter, – I had to leave my wife, very poorly in body and very agitated in mind, – this was painful to myself. At last, when I returned home on the 16th January I found her very unwell, – we all thought it a bad cold, – but she was no better when I left again and from that time became worse. The doctor was called in and Mrs. Lawson was with her and they all became alarmed. My son came to Stratford

F

on the Friday morning to tell me of his Mother's condition, but before I arrived at Brook Street her spirit had fled, – January 22nd.

It was indeed solemn and awful. As the doctors could not assign the cause of death I consented to a post mortem examination, at which there were three doctors, and Mrs. Lawson was present at the time, when it was found that the immediate cause of death was abcess of the stomach and as the abcess had broken about nine days previously, they were astonished that she had lived so long.

To her relatives it was more satisfactory to know, and Mrs. Swan had repeatedly desired that her body should thus be opened, – of course not knowing what ailed her, – but her suffering had been so distressing and almost maddening in effect at times. Poor creature, to be stricken down by disease at forty-five years only. But the poor soul, – alas, she never confessed to a fault, or said 'God be merciful, to me, a sinner'.

Thus I was called upon to part with the wife of my youth and the mother of my children.

On the Sunday week following, the body was interred at West Hackney Churchyard Stoke Newington Road, – all the children, myself and relatives following to the grave. January 31. 1858.

I was then working at Stratford, which lasted some months. My eldest went out to work at ironing, and Margaret being lame, yet done all the work of the house, the lads at work, and Martha who was now only recovering from the fever, soon after got a place of service, and Philip was attending school where he became a good writer and arithmetician. Thus we tried to work our way, and indeed we requir'd to, for I was left quite £20 in debt. But in course of time I was enabled to pay it, and those to whom it was owed waited until I could pay, and then we got some more home comfort.

I might have said, – I had a little difficulty with Mrs. Lawson. Having been with her sister at the time of her death, she left her work and wanted to fix herself in my home. In consequence I came home from Stratford one very cold night to see that she left and thereby got a cold and illness which lasted three weeks, – and Mrs. Lawson returned to her work.

1859. If I recollect aright, I was taken on again in the Spring at Newington until the fall of the year, then out-doors again. So we went on peacefully, the daughters industrious and the lads at work, Harriet managing house and going out, ironing, and Margaret doing the house work, Martha at service, and William at Tottenham, (gardening), Richard at the cowkeepers where he got as hearty as a young farmer, Philip at school. We all felt the benefit of health and industry.

1860. Began at out doors work, and I think, I went on at the shop again about Easter until October, but not full time, – this was more or less of a trial to me for I ought, according to the business, to have been on when I was told to be absent. Also I was not sure of success at the other. If I had obtained work in the City at my business, it would be in the cellars at many places and I should have suffered in my health, being always subject to Asthma. But what a compensation in God's goodness that I had so much employ in the suburbs of London, and the family brought up in an healthy locality...

Being out doors, and things slack, on October 20th, I went to Barclay's brewhouse carrying malt, a small job and would only fetch a shilling. It being a fine dry day, as I walked up the street from on board the barge, with a sack of malt on my back, my right foot slipped from under me and I fell with the sack on me. I very badly sprained the right ancle and lower part of the leg, yet it was a mercy I did not break the small bone of the leg. A brother freeman carried the sack up for me, but altho there were near a hundred freemen at the job, not one shewed me any other kindness. But a stranger seeing the hobbling condition I was in got me a broomstick, and a phial of horse oils from the stables of the brewhouse.

After some time I moved on with the stick and by the walls of the houses, through Boro Market, – thinking to get on a bus and get home, – arrived at the Boro a cabman helped me cross the road, and someone said as I hobbled along, – 'I would look in at the Hospital St. Thomas.'

This verse was brought to my mind, –
'Friend of the friendless and the faint
Where shall I lodge my deep complaint?
Where but with thee whose open door
Invites the friendless and the poor ...'

And so I found it. I went to the gate, was let into a room, doctors came and asked questions, pinched the leg and ancle, and said, – 'You must come in'. They sent two men to carry me upstairs and I was assisted to bed. It being Saturday afternoon I had just time to send the news to my family, – and they could see by my writing that my right arm was not hurt.

Attended by the House Surgeon until Monday when Dr. Solly examined more closely and said, – 'That is a precious bad sprain but I don't think there is any fracture of the small bone of the leg.' I was kept lying on my back for a fortnight with wet cloths to my leg day and night and a cradle over it. I had every attention I required and thro mercy felt cheerful in mind.

Mr. Palmer, Mr. Bond and other friends came to see me, and the Homerton friends were kind in assisting us, also Mrs. Chase collected of neighbours and Mr. Gamble's people, of £1. 5 shillings which paid my rent for five weeks, – the time I was in. I certainly enjoyed some happy hours in the hospital.

November 20th I was dismissed, but could only walk with crutches, – in about three weeks got on my leg again and got some work at the shop during the winter, but I was part time in and part time out doors.

1861. At the shop in spring and summer. . . In May, through kind information tendered by Mrs. Chancellor, my Philip was taken into the offices of Messrs Rickett Smith & Co., Stepney, at 5/- per week. Which was a help and yet a struggle at first to get him decent clothes. But his aunt kindly lodged him for a while and the second and third years his wages were advanced, and he was attentive. Coming home on Saturday evenings and returning on Monday mornings, he kept to Sunday School and Chapel very regular.

Although I was most tolerable in health, I had sore and painful boils and abcesses. I think the greater part of this year I was at the shop.

1863. Still mostly at the shop. . . At my Harriet's request, I had consented to her taking some washing in prior to this, on the understanding that it should be taken to her own place when she could get an home. In June, Harriet made a start for herself at Homerton, and about Michaelmas was married to James Port. Margaret continued with me to keep house, but was desirous to go and live with her sister if I should marry, – of which there was probability by this time.

1864. Continued at the shop, and now the family being all employed, and having been for some time in affectionate correspondence with Emma Herbert, many years a member at Hom Row, – and I trust it was of the Lord's leading and guidance for we both made it a matter of earnest prayer, – (My friend had been nurse in Doctor Dauglish's family fourteen years), on March 14th we were married at Homerton Row Chapel. I never regretted it since. But sorry to say there was room for much better feelings in some of my family towards us, – but youth is not always considerate.

Margaret went to live with the Ports as she had wished to do a long time. Philip only lodged at home on Saturday and Sunday evenings, but soon he became so ungrateful to Mrs. Swan and myself that I was glad when he took himself away to Harriet's.

Thus in the goodness of God I was united to a good partner, – having waited above six years and the Lord preserved me from evil, for I can truly say that during my solitude I never embraced another woman.

In July my William was married to a respectable young woman of Clapton.

I had only been united six months when again I was called to bear the cross of want of work, while all the others were kept on, – this being very unfair treatment. Through the interposition of Doctor Dauglish the next thing offered was some work for the Aerated Bread Company at Whitecross Street, City, – which though it was dirty drudgery work it lasted through the winter, and a very long one it was. . . Wages only £1 per week. So we moved to New North Street, Finsbury. At last obliged to leave the little house in Brook Street where I had lived for the greater part of twenty years.

While in town attended the ministry of Mr. G. Wyard, Lever St. St. Luke's under which, and in the society of his people, we both enjoyed the comforting presence of the Lord in whose hands are all our times.

1865.

In April I left the Bread Company and the following week was at work in Stratford at Cross Buns, but only got one week, then a week or two at the waterside. . .

Next sent for me to have part-time at Newington so moved back there to apartments in Church Street.

In May went on full-time, I think, – the close of the year, – but then a sore had broken out on my right leg which had always been weaker than the other from the time of the bad sprain in '60.

O what dependent creatures we are, for if one part fail we soon find our helplessness. But God had given me a kind companion to minister to my necessities, and Mrs. Daughlish was kind in her gifts of clothing to us, articles of clothing left off by the doctor etc., as also was Mr. Wright kind, father to Mrs. Daughlish.

1866.

Kept on at the shop until in the summer my leg became so bad I was obliged to lay up and lost six or seven weeks' work, then I went on again, but with so many changes that I cannot call them all to mind. The Lord has always supplied our wants, and preserved me from fire and flood unto the present moment.

'Bless the Lord O my soul, and forget not all his benefits who forgiveth all thine iniquities.'

In March 68 my Philip was married to M. A. Eaton of Clapton.

I was enabled to work through this year although I lost some time at the end and also in the summer Mrs. Swan was at Wimbledon at Mrs. Daughlish's, where she inhaled the stench of the drain and suffered an alarming attack of diarrhoea and fever so that her life was despaired of. Mrs. D. was very kind, anxious and attentive and had a first rate doctor come all the time required, – in fact everything that kindness and sympathy could do was done during the month. It pleased God to bless the means, and my partner was raised up again and spared to be an help to me.

Although returning home very weak, yet Mrs. D. was very kind to have nursed her at Wimbledon but that was because she had recieved the injury there.

About this time my Martha was married to Charles Sparrow.

During the spring and summer was at the shop. In July removed to Sanford Lane where we got an house at a low rent but had to do repairs, – and again I was on short time towards the end of the year, but still had much reason to be thankful for the kindness and gifts of Mrs. Daughlish to Mrs. Swan...

1870.

At the beginning I was subject to a good deal of weakness of body, yet for the most part was enabled to keep at the shop tho' suffering with a wound in my right leg. Now this proved to be an unusually hot and dry spring and summer and as the heat increased, (and which lasted from May until September), so the weakness and debility took more hold of me, so that on June 6th I was obliged to leave off work. Was quite enfeebled with the extreme heat, also great pain in my sore leg, and withal the spirits much depressed.

I was attending the Dispensary but the doctors gave but faint hope of relief saying I wanted change of air. I went on thus during June and July, the heat continued very oppressive, without rain.

At length, through the perseverance of Mrs. Swan we obtained of Mr. Jacomb of Clapton, a letter of admission to the Convalescent Hospital, Seaford, Sussex, for a month's residence, there, – at the sea-side.

Now I had been so weak on my legs and feet during two months that I could only creep out of doors. However Philip was moved to help me a little, (and he was now very prosperous and could well afford it), when the day came for me to go to Seaford, Philip and Mr. Eaton, his father in law, met us at London Bridge and paid my carriage to London and to Seaford, went there with me and gave me £1 which was the charge for my board and lodging in the hospital for one month.

Altho I had been despairing that I should ever recover strength again, – so, the Lord appeared for me. When I was got into the train the words were brought to my mind, – with great sweetness, –

'Fear not, I am with thee, O be not dismayed, I am Thy God.'

And so I found, in the goodness of God.

The Home was very comfortable and the food good and sufficient, and fine weather all the time and nothing to do but walk about and enjoy the beautiful air.

I was soon much benefitted and my leg healed.

Alas, altho all there were friendly, yet I could not find a Christian companion among the fifty, male, inmates.

At the month's end I returned, much improved in health but it was towards the end of the year before I regained my wonted strength.

I had a few days work when nearly Christmas, but the Lord supplied our wants, Christian friends were kind and others also, and the Lord brought us through that time of trouble. He did not fail or forsake us.

That September my Richard was married to Janet Felix.

1871. During this year my health was tolerably good. I had about two thirds at the shop (part time) for the rest I had to do the best I could and did a bit at the waterside although not strong enough for much of that.

In February '72 I obtained a gift of £2 from the Founders Company which most probably would have been more in amount but that I had never paid my dues to the company, – 2/- per year. At this time Philip was very prosperous in his situation and I therefore asked him to assist me by paying my dues for me, in hope of future benefit, but he refused.

At the shop, spring and summer and until November, part time, when fearing I should be quite off, applied at Stratford and was engaged to go on there on the 1st December, but in that fortnight interval my leg broke out in a sore, – which led to a deal of trouble.

Now it was not that I was wanted at Stratford, – I mean that they were not so busy, – but the master shewed favour to me, – well I had not been on a fortnight when the health of a man failing at the City shop of the Governor's and at the work I was most used to, – they desired me to supply his place, which I did for about two weeks, then he returned and so I returned to Stratford, (thus ended the year), – but changes awaited in my path.

In the early part of January, this same man, Rodney, became worse and died, – of bronchitis, – and I was desired to take the work, which I did, though very unwilling to work in that cellar in the City, knowing my health must suffer. As it did, and the wound in my leg grew larger and more painful, and I soon became very weak, and winter time withal. . . .

Now I had removed to Station Street Stratford before the man died, hoping to be at work there, not knowing I should be sent to the City, – thus leaving the house and garden at Newington to go into apartments in the damp and unhealthy locality of Stratford, but I DONE IT IN THE HOPE OF MORE EMPLOYMENT.

Of old, the Lord led Israel up and down the wilderness . . . the poet says, – 'He led their feet far wandering round, but 'twas the right way to Canaan's ground', and, thro mercy, I hope to reach that inheritance that is incorruptible and undefiled.

As well as I could I kept on at the City at work, going

to and fro morn and night, but I became very weak and suffered much with pain in my ulcerated leg.

But now was called to bear another trial in March, – it had happened that I was obliged to apply to Philip for help in illness and from want of work, (he was able, his income was very good,) and he had assisted me to remove and was then very friendly, but one morning on leaving home I advised Mrs. Swan to go to Stepney to see Philip and his wife, and nothing particular then did we notice. . . but alas he indulged to excess in strong drink. . .

I did not gain much strength in the atmosphere of Stratford during the remainder of the year '73, neither did I obtain any employ at the shop, another man doing the work I left.

In May '73 my Margaret was married to Benjamin Brace, by which I had the pleasure of living to see all three sons and all three daughters married, but I also bore the contempt of being absent from each of their weddings, my presence not being desirable. I could not help thinking, 'If I be a father where is my honour?'

But God sets one thing over against another and considering I was left a widower with three daughters and three sons not one brought disgrace upon me, – which is the sad lot of some parents.

This was an eventful year. In May, Mr. Palmer the minister of Hom Row died, having been there nearly twenty years.

In October my brother Thomas died after eight months illness, aged fifty eight. Sorry to say he did not like my company . . . I fear his was not a happy end, from all that I could gather, and knew of him.

Having been unable to work since April we became

straightened in our means by the summer and had to pledge clothes for necessaries.

Christian friends were kind, and also fellow workmen at Newington sent me a little help. Philip was unwilling to assist me, even to a refusal, although he could well afford it, – but at Christmas to my surprise a Mr. Jarvis, foreman in the bakehouse at Stratford, started a subscription for me because of my adversity and raised the sum of three guineas, and sent it to me without the least knowledge on my part of anything of the kind, – it was contributed by the workmen and others who had known me in years past.

Thus again the Lord supplied our wants, but I continued very weakly in body and I think the low damp atmosphere of Stratford was against me and promoted depression of spirits. During the time we were at Stratford we attended a good deal at a Baptist Chapel at West Ham Lane, a Mr. Bracher being the affectionate and faithful pastor, a friendly, brotherly man. There we had good counsel and company.

In January '74 by entreaty and the foreman's help, I got taken on at the shop, on at the marmalade work, as a labourer earning about 24/- per week, which lasted about six weeks, and then no more.

During this time we had to make another removal into the next street, leaving because of the conduct of the woman holding the house, but still worse in Martin Street, that there we found the Mrs. Smith to be an immoral character. A married man constantly visiting and the husband not ignorant of it, here was a disgraceful dilemma.

The early part of this year I suffered much weakness and debility and did just the six weeks at marmalade, but with much exhaustion and distress. When done I hoped to get some work in the bake-house but was disappointed, and withal had much despondancy of mind for I seemed shut out every way... looked and asked for a job, anything and everywhere, but all in vain.

Altho I enjoyed the Sabbath days and often got a cheering word at West Ham I suffered much distress of mind at other times because the prospect appeared so gloomy for the future. No doubt the common adversary of souls worried my mind greatly and very frequently about this time I was tempted to destroy myself.

O the vile suggestions of Satan, – after so much mercy past. At length it pleased God to give me a measure of returning health, about April, and we had a mild and pleasant spring so that I could get the benefit of the air.

Mrs. Daughlish and her daughters were kind to us, my William had sent some help at times and Richard once gave me 6/- but Philip who could best afford to do it was unwilling to help me further altho receiving a large income. I confess it is very humbling to a father to require help of his children but my family knew how much I earned and how I had spent the same and also the reverses I had been called to endure, with never robust health and also subject to Asthma. But thank God the family were for the most part healthy and all industrious. – 'The Lord will give strength to his people, The Lord will bless his people with peace, also unto the upright there ariseth light in the darkness...'

In the month of March Mrs. Daughlish seeing our adversities wrote to Philip, proposing to assist Mrs. Swan to a certain amount if Philip and his brothers would contribute to the same amount, to this Philip consented after a little delay, as it was a matter of policy to consent as William and Richard agreed to the same. This being arranged I of course considered a great boon yet still knowing the continuance or permanency of the whole rested on the ability and willingness of my sons to perform their part.

As the sequel will show. . . . Of the bounty of Mrs. Daughlish I had no cause to fear for such was her esteem and respect for us not withstanding the reverses we had met with.

However this was a supply and a relief for the present, – not that I wished to lay aside as an invalid. Towards the end of May there came a note from Stoke Newington, quite unexpected, that I could have a little work there if I would come at once. Of course I delayed not to go the same hour, thank God, I was feeling better in health, and with a thankful heart, and thinking it was a door opened for us again in God's good providence, I was again enabled to work. I had long desired to get away from Stratford.

In June we removed to Brighton Road, Stoke Newington and I felt cheerful to get back, I had endured so much at Stratford it seemed a blunder on my part when I applied for work there.

Now the Governor would not promise me much, but getting a little work and removing to Stoke Newington directly Philip and Richard endeavoured to excuse themselves from assisting me, – yet knowing the uncertainty of Volkman work, – but William continued to pay me. I was kept on until the end of August and was enabled to bear the heat and labour, thank God.

For some time prior to this, there had been different ministers supplying at Hom Row, where we had so long been united to the church, – but the members were too fickle to make choice of a good man, tho they had had several such among the supplies. Came one, William

Lodge, a man altogether unsuitable for ministry, – Now the deacon Mr. B., being the deacon with most money in his pocket determined to place him in the pastor's office, and the other deacons were content to let him do so. They therefore, after it had been settled at a meeting that he should supply the pulpit for another three months, in the most unfair and arbitary way called another meeting to push him in, altho it was objected to by several members, myself included. Because of the hasty manner of the course taken, and the whole of the church not knowing the proceeding, they drove on with the affair and managed to clap him in office.

He was the most coarse and ill-educated man I ever heard presume to speak from a pulpit. There was neither reverence, instruction or edification in his talk, for sermons I do not call them, – but noise and clamour, concept of self and censure of others were the points upon which he prided himself. Also in making food for fun in sacred things he was adept. Now I was sure this would not do, it was dishonouring to God. Having tried for some time to hear him, I was obliged to leave Hom Row, – but before leaving I told him that his preaching was not according to the word of God, to which he replied that it was a personal dislike on my part... quite untrue, for I had to do with him as a preacher, as a pastor.

He continued at Homerton Row, but there was no improvement in his preaching. We went chiefly to Mr. Vaughan's, Hackney, a preacher sound in the truth and chaste in his language, and instructive in his discourses. (I venerate such men.)

In '74, having been more prosperous, in September I went to Manchester to see my son (William) and wife and family, the which I had long desired to do. I had never been so far from London before, stayed six days inclusive, and very much enjoyed the time. I saw the master's house and estate, Manchester, Salford etc. and also saw the order of my son's house and family, had pleasant and safe journeys to and fro, and fine weather. Truly Manchester is a great city of trading and traffic with broad thoroughfares and noble buildings and institutions and with great facilities of conveyance to the wide spread suburbs and surrounding parks and gardens, – while one beholds in such a city the great numbers of business men and well to do persons it is lamentable to see so much of squalor and wretchedness in some streets, and the scores of almost naked, shoeless children.

1875.

In the early part got part time at the shop. Now was greatly grieved to witness the gross misconduct of my eldest daughter and her husband, they living in Brook Street, but which I should not have known had we remained in Stratford, – not to the extent of it, – but it continues a disgrace and reproach to her relatives. But the consequences must fall upon themselves. . .

Now, (having removed to Battens, Brook Street), I had a large garden to walk in this summer, and felt the benefit of such a treat, in God's providence. Was kept on at the shop until August, and had some part-time towards the end of the year. In November obliged to remove again, on account of Batten's son and daughter coming back to the apartments we held, – moved to Park Street, Church Street, S. N. Altho the rooms were small we took them as being the best we could afford, and being near the shop. Stoke

G

Newington is so much altered now, there is scarcely any small houses to be had, but many pulled down.

The day after Christmas my dear wife had a painful attack of rheumatism or gout and was so weak I had to fetch Dr. Cook. She kept to her bed about a fortnight and then it was about three weeks more to get on the foot, – I being at home did the nursing and domestics as well as I could. It was well it did not happen before. I had been three times operated upon this year for the inner part of the nose being cut, for polypus growing there. Done gratuitously, thank God.

Our times include many changes, now the people were getting dissatisfied with the preaching of William Lodge, and began to look about for the absentees. So knowing this I went to an evening service, when a deacon said to me 'We are appointed to visit you and Mrs. Swan.' Accordingly I went to his house, – being on short time, and also to suit them, – to converse about our non-attendance. Arrived there on the evening fixed and had about an hour's talk with Brother Fowler and Brother Absolem. Told them our mind fairly and the occasion of our absence, talked it over without anger or ill feeling, apparently, – although I told them there was neither instruction nor becoming spirit in W. Lodge's preaching, and also complained of the coercion of Mr. Barmore in forcing him upon the church and also of their consenting to the same notwithstanding the advice of several members, – all of which they could not deny nor contradict. So we parted friendly.

Hearing soon of the next church meeting I went to service and stayed, – could soon see Lodge and the deacons puzzled at my presence. An old member to help them asked if I were a member now, to which the secretary and a deacon replied

in the affirmative, – but I had better withdraw, he added.
I would not consent to withdraw. After waiting, whispering
etc., the secretary said, 'Your business was not coming on
this evening.' 'Then I certainly need not withdraw,' I said.

So they were baffled by their own false proceeding. The
old member seeing this, proposed adjournment, and Finch
seconded. Lodge put it to the vote, and it was carried.
I afterwards told Lodge and the secretary that they had
done me an injustice inasmuch as they had closed the
meeting rather than let me hear the Visitors' report. I
charged the secretary to make a faithful record of it.

I did not wish for strife so did not attend the next
meeting, but of course we were withdrawn, for non-
attendance, of which they sent a notice adding thereto, –

'We pray you may be preserved in the truth and practice
of the word, as you have been for many years.'

This was in March, and I felt I had only done my duty,
and I thank God I was enabled to do it. I told Lodge his
ministry would come to naught. In June he resigned.

Thus were we and many others driven from the house
of God where we had enjoyed the means of grace. It is
very bad for a church when money rules.

In June because of the smallness of the rooms in Park Street
we removed to Nursery Place, Stoke Newington, and felt
thankful to get there. The following six weeks being unusually hot even for July and August, – I was enabled to
stand the heat thank God, – we got more air by our removal
than we possibly could have done in Park St. Going now
frequently to unite in the worship of God at Little Alice
Street Chapel, and by the permission of the deacons and pastor

receiving with the church the ordinance of the Lord's supper.

The church and the pastor having heard of Homerton Row and William Lodge, one Sunday morning Mr. Masterton asked me if I would like to be proposed for membership to which I replied in the affirmative. After some conversation with two of the deacons and after attending their next church meeting at which the Lord enabled me in a brief manner to tell the church of the gracious dealing of the Lord to my poor soul, – under the ministry by Mr. Shenston first and in that chapel when I was a lad of 17, and how tho in much distress of mind because of the guilt of my sins, brought home to me I trust by the Holy Spirit, how the Lord delivered me, under the ministry of Mr. Curtis of Hom Row at the age of 34, giving me forgiveness of sins through the atonement of Jesus Christ, – and also I was able to speak of the comfort and support I had enjoyed since that happy time, in times of trouble and affliction.

'And' said the pastor, 'You have been at Hom Row ever since?'

'Yes' I said, 'under the ministry of Mr. Curtis and Mr. Palmer, – but I could not hear the next man,' and so I ended my tale. After a space for the church to consult, and that very short, I was received. On a Sunday in July I was publicly received in the church. And I trust it was of the Lord that I felt constrained to go to Alice Street Chapel, because of the truth preached there although the distance at my time of life seemed to oppose the course I took. Yet love to the society, knowing several of the friends, and being desirous of the friendship of the people of God, and also in some humble measure to contribute to the cause of God and of truth – these were the reasons which prompted the steps I took.

I was at work at the shop this summer until the third week in September when having an attack of a bowel complaint I was obliged to stay away a few days, – of which Volkman took the advantage and I got no more work that year, except for one week before Christmas Day.

In September My Philip left a very lucrative employment, where he had been upwards of fifteen years, not for dishonesty, but being too proud and haughty, and indulging to excess in drink, of which he had been told and reproved for repeating, and yet continuing the same course. He, in a bad state one day demanded more salary and that being refused, instantly he resigned. How sad to see a son lose a good situation, producing more than £500 per annum, and at first he was not willing to acknowledge his folly.

1877 *January*.
Began this year without any employment, but have much to be thankful for, having things necessary to the body, – and this at a time of great distress to many people by reason of long, continuous and heavy rains, with gales and floods and storms, destroying much property and rendering many localities unfit for habitation, and also causing the employment of many to discontinue for a time.

Thus I thank God I have been enabled to perform my promise to my son William which I made some time since to record some of the changes I have passed through.

'Bless the Lord, O my soul, and forget not all his benefits.'

And as to my mortal body, I am spared in a measure of health and strength, looking forward to the 64th anniversary of my natal day. Notwithstanding the close confinement to the workshop of my business and the long hours exacted, having been subject to Asthma from my youth, the toils and trials and at times the sicknesses I have been enabled to bear, – having obtained mercy and help from the Lord, I have continued to this day, January 9th 1877. Thus the Lord has enabled me remember and record some of his goodness to a poor sinful creature, and although his mercy is new every morning and his faithfulness is so great, yet we do not notice and consider as we should. His constant care and continued goodness, promises help all the days of our pilgrimage.

I will try to record some things each month. . .

January. Continued all the month out of work, and a winter of rains and floods for three months. I suffered with Scurvied head, having a deal of hard scabby matter covering the skin for which I am attending Dr. Kellock and find some relief by the end of the month.

Philip made an attempt at business as a coal merchant at Limehouse, also Richard has been a shopkeeper at Limehouse during the last two years, he has been unwell for the last four months with a cankered mouth and throat and tongue.

I am sorry to have to notice that he has failed to perform his word wherein he promised three years ago to assist me to the amount of 1/6 per week, although he has had the ability to do it, he has not done so during the past 27 months.

Through mercy, I am enabled to attend the house of God and enjoy the worship and the friendship of the people of God. Thanks be to God.

February. Kept out of work all this month, altho applied

2 or 3 times, asking for part-time. In tolerably good health, thank God. And with medicine and salve from the Dispensary under Dr. Kellock find my head very much relieved of the Scurvy, the scabby state it was in six weeks ago. How beneficent of my Heavenly Father following upon the ailment to send the means of relief gratuitously.

My poor sister, Mrs. Stevens, who six months ago suffered with a third attack of paralysis which rendered her weak and helpless and speechless, and her husband being so reduced in circumstances by his family troubles and afflictions was necessitated to take her to the parochial infirmary on the 21st, – at Edmonton. Her poor body is very much wasted of flesh and at times her mind is quite delirious, but her shrieks and screams and cries are very distressing, – being quite helpless it is very sad to witness. And poor thing, how painful for her to endure. O Lord grant her thy merciful interposition, and her husband thy support.

While it has been trying to my faith and patience to be so long out of work, (now five months except one week at Christmas), I have to be thankful God gave me so good a wife, who is frugal and careful of every sixpence, or we must have been in distress. Also I thank God for his gracious and comforting presence and support, so I live to prove.

'The young lions do lack and suffer hunger, but they that seek the Lord shall not want any good thing.'

March.
Continued tolerably in health, thank God and whereas

Mrs. Swan and myself suffered an attack of rheumatic pain in the early part of last year we have been exempt this year so far, thank God. I have had a fortnight's work at the shop, also this month Good Friday and Easter falling early this year I hope to be kept on part-time, and I trust the Lord will give me strength according to my day.

The Scurvy humour which attacked my head has nearly gone under the treatment of Dr. Kellock, with the blessing of God, but there is a little weakness remaining in the eyes, but surely I ought to be grateful.

April. Continued in tolerably good health, thank God, altho it was a month of of very cold North East winds. Also I had part time at the shop.

May. Through the blessing of God, continued in good health although this also was a month of cold North East winds. I dont know whether I ever knew so cold a month of May. Also I had a good share of work. Mrs. Swan has been but very poorly for some weeks past.

Thus I was spared to see the 64th anniversary of my birthday on the 17th of this month, and though I have 3 daughters and 3 sons not one of the number sent me a word of remembrance on the occasion, (true they are all married and have their own cares and anxieties, and they are not burdensome to me).

June. With this month we had three weeks of very hot weather and enabled to bear the change, – but Mrs. Swan was very poorly. I had a good share of work. My son Richard was very ill of ulcerated throat. My daughter

Margaret had another boy, making a total of seventeen grandchildren, living.

July. Very busy at the shop this month. I was enabled to make full time and over. When I look back I am sure I ought to record the goodness of God to me, which brings to remembrance a circumstance of nearly 14 years ago, – when in distress and with an empty pocket I returned home having met with great unkindness from a son, – as soon as I reached home and entered my bedroom this passage was brought to my mind with great sweetness, – 'But my kindness shall not depart from thee' Isaiah 54 chapter, 10 verse, and indeed the whole of the connection... O what a precious chapter that is, and I can truly say that the Lord has been as good as his word.

August. Continued in tolerably good health, thank God, and also had work for the month. What is more, Mr. Volkman became so generous that he promised to give each man a day's holiday in the summer of each year. So myself and Mrs. Swan went to Gravesend by water on the 13th, returned safely and had a pleasant day.

September. Continued in tolerably good health, thank God. I had only ten days work at the shop this month. Mrs. Swan very poorly all the month.

October. I had some work during three weeks of this month, there being one man away ill. Also Mrs. Daughlish in her usual kind and generous manner sent Mrs. Swan to a Convalescent Home at Brighton for three weeks, from whence she returned improved in health. Surely the mercies of the Lord . . . attend his household all their days.

November. Had no work this month. The weather very wet. On the 9th my sister Mrs. Stevens departed this life, having lain 15 months prostrated with paralysis, which rendered her quite helpless and speechless. Thus it pleased God to terminate her sufferings and griefs which were great, – although she could not communicate her feelings to others except by strong cries and screams and looks, – so very painful to witness and must have been agonising to herself. But thus having left a living testimony to the grace of God, for she was a godly woman, earth was exchanged for heaven. At the age of 53, her health had been declining for a long time, and subsequently debility, and excessive grief on account of the bad conduct of her daughters shook the poor mortal frame. But God in mercy, interposed, – and her husband and we, her relatives have a well-grounded hope of her eternal happiness. I followed to the grave at Enfield churchyard on the 15th, as did her husband and daughters, also three sisters and others.

O Lord prepare me for the solemn hour when thou will call me away from all that is mortal and changing.

December. Had no work this month, but being spared to see the close of another year I have much cause for thankfulness to my Heavenly Father, also through the year I have been favoured with some sweet seasons of the Lord's presence.

Albeit I had much occasion to grieve over some of the conduct of my family. As to bodily health, – tolerably well, but towards the end of the year again subject to the dry scurvy in the head and ears, also at times sore boils on different parts of the flesh. But it furnished matter for prayer for the grace of patience and faith to wait all the days of the appointed time,

> 'Then I hope to rise to a better land
> where no chilling winds or poisonous breath
> shall reach that healthful shore,
> sickness, sorrow, pain and death
> are felt or feared no more . . .'

> thanks be to God.

1878 *January*. A time of general depression of trade, although an unusually mild winter. I had no more work this month, also very uncomfortably situated in the apartments we held, and purposing to move on that account. Very unwell the last part of the month with a great boil on the lower part of my back which occasioned much pain and weakness.

February. As we had obtained apartments at 3 Cromwell Terrace, Church Street, we removed on the 11th, and it was that I had just enough strength for the job of moving – and the day after and for the next fortnight I was quite prostrated with a great carbuncle at the back of my neck. Thank God I was getting better by Sunday the 24th, – they sent for me to go to work on the 26th, which I could not have done during the fortnight prior to this, such was the weakness I suffered from the carbuncle. Yet I was enabled to work the four days I was wanted. 'The Lord knoweth the days of the upright.'

March. Begun with some days of work equal to a fortnight (with those worked in February), which I obtained through the illness of one, Fletcher. Of course no more after that, during the remainder of the month. But I had another sore boil on my neck, the last being the fourth in 5 months, and also the least of the four. I have been better in health since, so I prove The Lord is good, a stronghold in the day of trouble.

We had more winter this month than any other this season. . .

April. Toward the middle of the month a little work at the shop equal to a fortnight so making 4 weeks in 4 months. Very unkindly spoken to by the master because I complained of the unfairness and requested more consideration.

Lord, undertake for me, – thou hast said 'The needy shall not always be forgotten; the expectation of the poor shall not perish for ever.'

For a long time past I have grieved to see my Philip drink to excess, and although he had a good start and to appearance he might do well, at the present things look very doubtful. He will not take advice or warning from me, by word of mouth or by letter, – for I have tried both methods, but in vain.

May. During a long continuance of wet weather have kept tolerably well, thank God, except that I have had to submit again to operation 2 or 3 times by the cutting of the inner part of my nose. Had no work this month, except half a day at a bread baker's, but it was very plain. I was kept back by Volkman because I complained of unfairness and asked that they should give me a share of the work, as well as others. It makes the time drag on heavily with anxiety to myself and my partner who has been very poorly. But the Lord is our helper, – and I trust he ever will be.

On the 17th I arrived at my 65th anniversary of my birthday, – a long time to be the constant receiver of mercy and goodness and grace. I trust of my Covenant God . . . I must say, – 'Father I wait thy daily will, Thou shalt divide my portion still, grant me on earth what seems thee best, till death and heaven reveal the rest.'

June. With this month I began to get some work at the shop and although the weather was extremely hot I was enabled to bear the heat and do the labour, thank God.

Continued to be greatly grieved to see Philip giving himself up to drunkenness so that at times incapable of attending to business, and becoming debilitated in body. About the 19th his brother William being in London and not having seen Philip during the past ten years, desiring again to show his friendliness made an opportunity to call to see him at home, – but was grieved very much to find him insensibly stupid with strong drink. But he, William, only witnessed then what I have done many times for years past. I must feel persuaded in my mind that such a bad course must meet with God's displeasure and bring its own punishment, and I fear, bring him to an early grave.

July. During the greater part of this month at work at the shop. Weather very hot and stormy. . .

On the 6th I went to see Philip, he was very poorly but no worse than I had seen him lately. I remarked that it was his birthday anniversary and said, 'You are 31 to-day, but o how different to when you were 21' to which his wife sighed assent. He remained silent and sullen and would not converse about his condition, nor about his brother seeing him in the state he was in a short time before. This turned out to be the last time I should see him alive. O painful to record.

He grew worse from that time, but of which I was not aware, his wife paying every attention and the doctor in constant attendance. At last, about the 14th he took to his bed, only to be raised from it by assistance, also being insensible for 2 or 3 days and nights together, – the effect of the disease. During the first hour of the 24th he departed this life. Receiving a message to that effect I went to the house on the evening of the 24th and saw the poor body and the sad face. Also saw to the putting of the body into the coffin. But the poor soul, o alas alas, he never confessed a fault.

On the 27th he was buried in his own grave in Abney Park Cemetery, followed by his father and his brothers William and Richard, his uncle Chancellor, and his clerk F. Hagan, and Mr. Whitford, Hurrell and Besant.

The affectionate wife has done her best by him and by the family they had and now the poor thing I fear is left in debt. She has been wonderfully supported under her troubles for she has lost her mother and brother lately and has her father lying in dying circumstances.

August.
During the first part of this month especially I felt very much the death of my son. But I was supported under the sharp grief which every recollection of him brought.

On the 11th Mr. Eaton died (Philip's father-in-law), and his memory deserves respect, for by frugality and carefulness he had sufficient for himself in his last years and also some substance to leave his daughter now, in her time of need.

I was on work part-time up to the 15th and then no more this month.

September.
In tolerably good health but only had three days work this month, and that through the death of a man, – again a time of perplexity inasmuch as I have no prospect of work during the winter, and what little I received from Philip has of course ceased with his death.

October.
Still in health thank God, but kept without employment all the month which increased my anxiety concerning the supply of providence, – O Lord, give me faith to believe in thy care and goodness, and be pleased to direct my way again and appear for me.

November.
In tolerably good health yet with a stubborn cough and shortness of breath, and still kept without work which gave me much anxiety and often brought me to cry unto the Lord for his interposition.

December came and I feared I should close the year without any more work but on the 10th they sent for me at the shop to accomodate themselves, J. Smith being ill, – (he died on the 19th thus in less than 4 months two men died there). Just at this time very hard weather set in. Thus again our wants were supplied. Thank God for strength.

Mrs. Swan has been and continues very poorly and when lately at Wimbledon met with a deal of trouble through the envy and slander of a servant, – very grievous.

Thus we are spared to see another year, and O how great is our indebtedness to the goodness and mercy of God. Such an eventful year of calamities and loss of life by sea and land, and famine and war abroad.

I have followed my son and two fellow workmen to the grave (I had worked with the men many years). Although I have had to bear the loss of a deal of time, I have enjoyed very often the Lord's presence, and blessing through the means of grace and in the company of the dear people of God, also in visiting I have seen two aged men very HAPPY in the prospect of death, trusting in the Lord.

1879. *January*. Spared through the mercy and long suffering forbearance of my Heavenly Father to see the first month of a new year, and also beginning in some work. Surely I have much cause to be thankful, and the more so as we have just had 3 months of stern winter weather, a time of want and distress to many. We have been supported and supplied, but also felt the effects of cold and damp in bodily weaknesses.
But truly the Lord has showed me marvellous kindness,— and often heard my poor prayers. Bless the Lord, o my soul.

February. Favoured to be at work about two thirds of this month and enabled to perform the labour, this is more work than I have obtained in the month of February for some years past. And very helpful to us, – for the weather was wintry with frost and snow, – and depression of trade very general.

March. The latter part of which was extremely cold, keen winds and heavy falls of snow making the winter long and trying. At work the greater part of the month, thank God.

On the 26th my eldest sister, Mrs. Joyce departed this life, aged 71, but through mercy we sorrow not as those without hope. Having been the mother of a numerous family her life had been one of care and anxiety, poverty and suffering, but there was scarcely a word of complaint uttered and I am sure she loved the ways of the Lord and walked in them from her youth. O happy exchange of worlds, – after passing through great tribulations to dwell for ever with the Lord. Praise ye the Lord.

April. On the 5th made another removal, to Aldam Place, High Street, which we were obliged to make being placed so uncomfortably, and also constantly in danger of fire, – a carpenter's workshop on the ground floor and they very careless with the shavings and gaslight and matches, thank God we escaped unhurt, and we were able to get away altho it was a task.

At work the greater part of the month and enabled to do which was a help as other helps had failed, also the cold weather continued. Bless the Lord O my soul and forget not all his benefits.

May.
At work all the month and thank God enabled to do it. On the 17th arrived at the 66th anniversary of my birthday, – spared so long and so many mercies. What shall I

H

render to the Lord for all his kindness shown? O Lord give me a thankful heart and a cheerful submission to thy will.

June.

Again at work all the month. Also passed through a time of affliction, in that my dear partner suffered a violent attack of gout in both feet and ancles and legs so that I had to fetch a doctor, whose attendance and medicine was made useful, with poultices etc. The trial also fell in some measure upon myself, being the subject of rheumatic pains, possibly promoted by the continued wet weather. We have gone through 9 months of very trying and unusual weather up to this time with very little sunshine, the consequences are want of labour to many and general depression of trade. The continuous rain and storms occasion depression of the spirits, – and yet the writer has had more work and been enabled to do it (thus our Heavenly Father has supplied us) . . .

July.

Continued at work all this month and tolerably well myself but Mrs. Swan has suffered much during the last eight weeks and remains in a very weak state. The weather continues wet and cold until near the end of this month.

August.

Again continued in work all the month, thus we have been wonderfully helped the first eight months of the year, in God's good providence and bounty. Altho it has been a very rainy season I have had work and been enabled to do it yet not without a good deal of felt weakness of body and especially with rheumatic pains. Still I am supported and sometimes sweetly favoured with joy and peace in believing and verily of late I have proved that promise true, which the Lord gave his people by the mouth of Jeremiah when in Babylon, – 'Behold I will plead thy cause.'

My dear partner is a little better at the end of this month, and Mrs. Daughlish has been very kind as usual.

September.

Now began to get slack at work again, so that I have only had 13 days work this month. Feeling poorly I really wanted a little rest and desire to be thankful for what work I have had of late in God's good providence. Also my dear wife has improved in health and I hope will soon recover more strength.

On the 27th I went by rail safely to Manchester to spend a few days with my son and his wife and family. Richard also there by another train so that we met at Manchester without any previous intention. Very pleased to find all pretty well and in good order, the children are very happy, – so they ought to be for they are well cared for. The season has been very trying to my son in his garden but I did not hear of any complaint about it made by the master. Attended the preaching on the 28th at the Lecture Room, Baptist Chapel, Brighton Grove, Manchester, – but alas, I heard of duty, faith and good works, and but little of sovereign mercy and free grace.

October.

Returned by rail safely from Manchester on the 2nd, having had a pleasant stay of six days inclusive of travelling.

All the month without work and as far as I can see but

small prospect, because two of the grandsons have come to the work. One thing I should have noticed, meeting with Richard at Manchester I had a better chance of telling him how I was situated, in consequence he said he wanted to do a little for me, say 1/6 per week, of which I received the first part on the 20th. My daughter-in-law at Manchester said, concerning our meeting there, – 'depend upon it, there is something in it.'

I have felt better in health this month for truly I was very poorly at the end of last month. But tis our God supports our frame, the God who built us first. . .

November.
Again had to pass the month without any work. Some very wintry weather from the middle of the same. Appearances rather depressing and it has often been the same, as soon as they can do without me at the shop I have to lose time while mostly all the others are kept on. But with my God I leave my cause and trust his promised grace.

December. Wintry weather continuing. Sent for at the shop and had nearly seven days work before Christmas Day, this being the last this year. Thus brought to the close of another year, looking back I have cause for thankfulness, I have had more work this year than in some preceeding ones and I really needed the money.

Whether I shall be spared to record another year's events or no I must leave in the Lord's hand, but I trust the Lord is and will be my salvation in life and in death also.

1880. January.
Spared to see the beginning of another year which has

come in with very trying weather, hard frosts at times and many days and nights of dense fogs during this month. Had no work, but as to health, tolerably thank God.

February.

Having been advised by a brother freeman (of the Clothworkers Company) to apply to my company for some pecuniary help, on the 9th I presented a petition which I was very successful in getting signed by six gentlemen, – it was well received and I obtained a gift of £5 at Founders Hall, City. Now this came very seasonably, as this is the 5th month without work save seven days, and this repays the £7 it cost to take up my freedom (£2 I received in 1872). Thank God for his manifold mercies.

My dear partner requested by Mrs. Daughlish to go to Norwood to mind a house being repaired and refurnished to let again. Such was the condition of everything that Mrs. S. had a very toilsome and distressing time of it.

March.

After the first fortnight had passed I had some work at the shop from the 15th. Also on the 20th Mrs. Swan came home from Norwood. Certainly it was well for us that the job was over for her late mistress had been severe and unkind in this instance, requiring more than she or any one else could accomplish. This was nothing but an imposition knowing very well we had received many kindnesses from her. It was quite three weeks before Mrs. Swan recovered her usual measure of health.

But in this way we were led and supported, with strength sufficient for the day.

'The Lord his saints supplies, this thought
  Should keep them from dismay,
    Though many foes arise. . .
  . . . The Lord will bring them through. .'
Praise ye the Lord.

Philip Swan lies buried in his own grave, No. 45569
proceeding from the gates in High Street, go to the right
hand path and pass the Grotto a little space in the 4th row
of graves between the path and the wall; having the names
of Dubois on the right and Little on the left.